THE POWER OF EXPECTATION

THE POWER OF EXPECTATION

E.C. NAKELI

King's Word Publishing

© 2015 by E.C. Nakeli

Published by King's Word Publication

For your questions and publishing needs, write to:

>E.C. Nakeli
>40 S Church st
>Westminster, MD 21157
>E-mail: *ecnakeli@yahoo.com*

Printed in the United States of America

All rights reserved. No part of this publication may be reproduced, stored in a retrieval systems, or transmitted in ay form or by any means— for example, electronic, photocopy, recording—without the prior written permission of the publisher. The only exception is brief quotations in printed reviews.

E.C. Nakeli

To contact the author, write to:

>E.C. Nakeli
>40 S Church st
>Westminster, MD 21157
>E-mail: *ecnakeli@yahoo.com*

The Power of Expectation / E.C. Nakeli

ISBN: 978-0-9850668-9-5

>Unless otherwise indicated, Scriptures references are from
>THE HOLY BIBLE, NEW INTERNATIONAL VERSION®, NIV®
>Copyright © 1973, 1978, 1984, 2011 by Biblica, Inc™
>Used by permission. All rights reserved worlwide.

Cover Design: Zach Essama *-graphicspartner@gmail.com*

Interior Design: Zach Essama *graphicspartner@gmail.com*

Table of Contents

Intoduction 1
Chapter 1: Expectation Will Cause You not to Miss the Day of Your Visitation 5
Chapter 2: Expectation Will Point to You the Place of Your Life-changing Scarifice 9
Chapter 3: Expectation Will Cause You to See Your Miracle of Supernatural Provision ..11
Chapter 4: Expectation Will Cause You to Discover Your Secret to Breakthrough 15
Chapter 5: Expectation Will Prepare You for the Day of Adversity 19
Chapter 6: Expectation Will Boost Your Confidence..21
Chapter 7: Expectation Will Cause You to Behold God's Glory......................................25
Chapter 8: Expectation Will Cause You to see Your Way Cleared 29
Chapter 9: Expectation Will Cause You to Rise to New Heights 33
Chapter 10: Expectation Will Give You a Picture of Your Future....................................37
Chapter 11: Expectation Will Show You the Vastness of Your Inheritance 41
Chapter 12: Expectation Will Lead You to Repentance 45
Chapter 13: Expectation Will Bring About Your Restoration 49
Chapter 14: Expectation Will Give You Security and Safety 53
Chapter 15: Expectation Will Cause You to Receive Guidance.......................................57
Chapter 16: Expectation Will Cause You to Keep Your Integrity 59
Chapter 17: Expectation Will Cause You to Wait 63
Chapter 18: Expectation will Inspire You to Praise 65
Chapter 19: Expectation Will Generate
and Maintain Your Zeal for The Lord and His Kingdom..69
Chapter 20: Expectation Will Cause You to Rejoice 71
Chapter 21: Expectation Will cause You to Persist in Prayer 75
Chapter 22: Expectation Will Cause You to Endure 77

Chapter 23: Expectation Will Give You Stability and Firmness 81
Chapter 24: Expectation Will Move Your Heart Towards the Needy 83
Chapter 25: Expectation Will Cause You to Reap a Harvest 85
Chapter 26: Expectation Will Cause You to Excel 87
Chapter 27: Expectation Will Bring About Your Deliverance 89
Chapter 28: Expectation Will Cause You to Be Bold 91
Chapter 29: Expectations Will Bring About Your Expansion 93
Chapter 30: Expectation Will Move You Closer to God 95
Chapter 31: Expectation Will Cause You to Inherit God's Promises 97
Chapter 32: Expectation Will Keep You from Shame and Disappointment 99
Chapter 33: Expectation Will Cause 101
Chapter 34: Expectation Will Cause You to Be Raptured 103
Chapter 35: Expectation Will Open You to The Supernatural 105
Chapter 36: Expectation Will Reveal to
You Important People in Your Life and Ministry 109
Chapter 37: Your Expectation Will Cause You to Receive a Commission 111
Chapter 38: Expectation Will Enhance Your Spiritual Hearing Capacity......113
Chapter 39: Further Truths About Expectations 115
Chapter 40: Beware of Wrong Expectations 119

Introduction

Life becomes totally unfulfilling and void of true meaning when a vital ingredient to sustain it is lacking. The life that ceases to improve physically and more especially spiritually does so for one overriding reason. And the one who constantly improves and makes use of the opportunities God offers in different ways does so for only one reason.

On the one hand, the life that fails to improve does so for lack of expectations. On the other hand, the one that improves does so because of the ingredient called expectation. Expectation is the bedrock on which the edifice of faith is built. It is what provides a ground on which faith can be demonstrated.

A man or woman, boy or girl, will never rise to any level beyond his/her expectation. Be it spiritually, financially, socially, morally, mentally, physically or professionally, when there is no expectation there is no lasting or solid progress. If by chance anyone is raised beyond his/her expectations in whatever domain, he/she will automatically drop to the level where his/her expectations can sustain him/her.

The presence or absence of expectation in a life will determine the corresponding presence or absence of other essential qualities that constitute the driving force for life. Expectation, when present in your life will cause you to demonstrate faith and thereby move into the fullness of your inheritance in Christ Jesus.

An expectation can be concrete or abstract, right or wrong, true or false, strong or weak, bad or good. And every life moves in the direction of its expectations. You cannot go further than your expectations on this long road to your destiny. And you also cannot rise higher than your expectation in the realm of exploits. Some people build their life on the expectations of others. When this happens, fulfillment is not only lacking but frustration, anger, and a great sense of self-disappointment takes precedence.

You are holding this book in your hand because you want to understand the power that is in one's expectations. At a certain point in time I decided to watch my own life. After a period of eighteen months I came to realize that much depends on my expectations based on the word of God. When I didn't expect anything, nothing happened. When I expected little, little happened. When I expected much, much happened. Besides, in talking with others and in reading about others, I am yet to find one man who rose higher than or went farther than his expectations. That is what motivated me to write, *"The Power of Expectations"*, the right kind of expectations of course!

Operational definition of terms and expressions

Some basic terms and expressions employed in this book will be explained here, within the context our topic.

Expectation: It is defined in the life application study Bible as what you *"consider probable or certain; hope; assurance."*

We shall use that word expectation based on the word of God, in which case we will ignore probability and dwell only on the certainty spelt out in the above definition. Thus we narrow our definition of expectation to be *"what you consider certain"*.

Introduction 3

Hope: as defined in the same reference above is something desired with confident expectation of its fulfillment.

These two definitions give us the latitude to be able to use both words interchangeably as we will do throughout this work. Several Hebrew words are translated in the KJV of our Bible as Hope. However, such words have a broader meaning of trust, confidence, safety, refuge etc. One of such words as used in the Hebrew Old Testament is *"Sêeber"* (strong # 7664) which is translated as expectation or hope.

The Greek word for hope in the Greek New Testament is ĕlpis which means to anticipate with pleasure; expectation, confidence or hope.

Thus your expectation, based on what God has said is equivalent to hope. That is why we shall use both words interchangeably.

Lift up one's eyes: The phrase *"lifts up one's eyes"* whether in the present, past or future tense will also be used frequently. It is used to express expectation. Nobody lifts up his or her eye(s) except motivated by expectation.

Having explained these, I believe the ground has been prepared for you to aptly understand all that will be said in this volume.

Be ready to move further and rise higher by the time you go through this book. If you are contented with mediocrity or the status quo then close the book and hand it to someone who desires to improve. But I want to believe you are determined to go further and rise higher than where you are currently. May the Spirit of the Living God propel and lift you as you read through.

Your expectations will determine your input in the issues of life and consequently your output. Expectations also determine your investments and constraints of time, energy, money, and other resources. Your expectations will define your relationships, priorities, motivations and interests in life. There is tremendous power released in expectations.

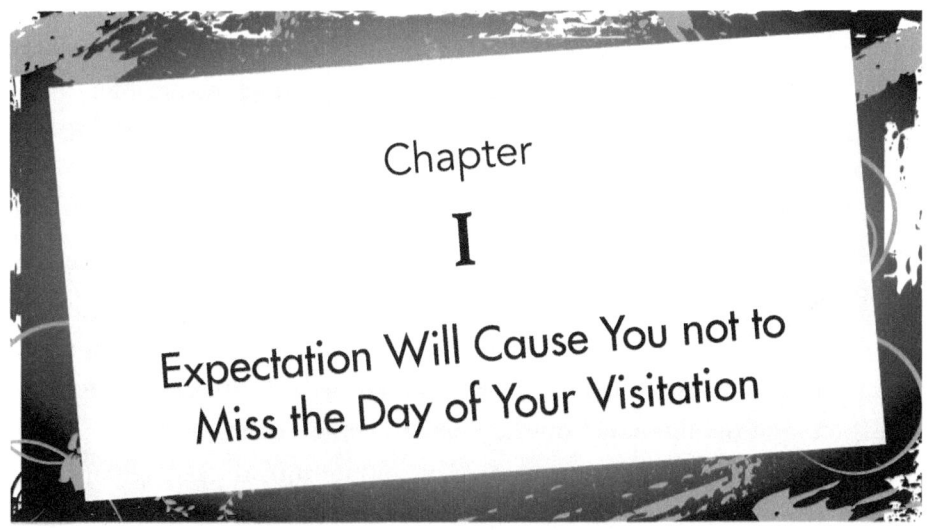

Chapter I

Expectation Will Cause You not to Miss the Day of Your Visitation

There are times when God decides to visit an individual, a people, a city or even a nation for blessing and to avert certain unpleasant happenings. Such seasons or days or moments are not common. When you miss your season, the whole purpose of your existence may be affected because there is no guarantee that it will repeat itself.

One thing that will help secure the day of your visitation (i.e. of God's coming to you) is the right expectation. The Lord Jesus Christ, weeping over the city of Jerusalem said: *"If thou hadst known, even thou, at least in this thy day, the things which belong unto thy peace! But now they are hid from thine eyes."* (Lk 19: 41-42 KJV).

The day of your visitation is the day God comes to you. When God comes to His child, it is to increase, enlarge, expand, elevate and bless. The time of God's coming to you is the time He offers you special access to His treasure house. It is the time when everything in your life which is not of Him is forced to take a permanent leave.

Like Jerusalem, nothing else but what happened to this beloved city when she missed the day of her visitation should be expected by anyone who follows in her footsteps. When you miss the day of your visitation, your enemy may gain the upper hand over you. Many things will go wrong in your life. In fact all what you may have built may crumble. May you never miss the day of your visitation!

Now what caused Jerusalem to miss her day of visitation? It is simple: she had the wrong expectation of how her king was to come and worse of all how He was to look. This caused her to reject the very One who was supposed to shield and protect her. Lack of expectation is bad but the wrong kind of expectation usually based on the illusions conceived in the human mind instead of God's word is even worse. May you not miss the day of your visitation, when God comes to you to preserve you, promote you, and position you for further blessings.

About Abraham, it is written *"The LORD appeared to Abraham near the great trees of Mamre while he was sitting at the entrance to his tent in the heat of the day. 2 Abraham looked up and saw three men standing nearby. When he saw them, he hurried from the entrance of his tent to meet them and bowed low to the ground."* (Genesis 18:1-2).

Look at that! *"Abraham looked up and saw…"*

This talks of nothing but expectation. The one who looks up automatically lifts up his eyes. Because of his expectations, Abraham did not miss the day of his visitation. I believe these angels were standing nearby but until Abraham looked-up, he did not notice their presence. In other words until Abraham had expectations he never took note of this life-changing, destiny-fulfilling visit of God.

Expectation is what causes you to lift up your eyes from yourself and grab the day of your visitation. Expectation has the capacity to keep you focused on the object of your expectation rather than being distracted by whatever. Live your life daily in anticipation of God's blessings upon you. Lack of this may cause you to by-pass or miss your blessings. Peter wrote to the saints urging them, *"Having your conversation honest among the Gentiles: that, whereas they speak against you as evildoers, they may be your good works, which they shall behold, glorify God in the day of visitation"* (I Pe 2:12, KJV).

The day of your visitation shall compel respect and honour from the unbelievers. They shall acknowledge you and glorify your God. Their language and opinion about you will change. In fact what their eyes have been blind to, regarding the glory of God in your life, they shall behold glaringly.

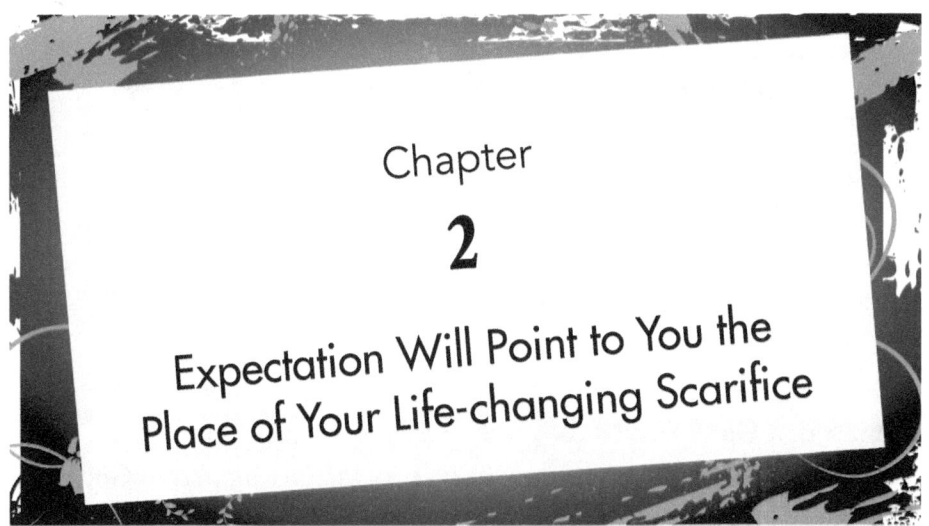

Chapter 2
Expectation Will Point to You the Place of Your Life-changing Scarifice

There is power in sacrifice, that is, the right kind of sacrifice in the right place. In fact the Father of all creation understands best the power of sacrifice. For that reason He chose to redeem renegade humanity through the ultimate sacrifice of His only Son, Christ Jesus in a specific city on a particular hill. Now expectation will not only cause you to discover the kind of sacrifice you need to make in order to orchestrate your breakthrough but will also show you the right place to make the sacrifice.

Some people, have discovered the kind of sacrifice to make but by failing to discover the right place have been eluded by the breakthrough they were searching for.

Abraham, when asked by God to sacrifice his only son Isaac, who was born to him twenty-five years after the promise was made, did not hesitate to obey because of the expectation he had. It is written:

> *1 "Some time later God tested Abraham. He said to him, 'Abraham!'*
> *"Here I am," he replied.*

> ² Then God said, "Take your son, your only son, Isaac, whom you love, and go to the region of Moriah. Sacrifice him there as a burnt offering on one of the mountains I will tell you about."
> ³ Early the next morning Abraham got up and saddled his donkey. He took with him two of his servants and his son Isaac. When he had cut enough wood for the burnt offering, he set out for the place God had told him about.
> ⁴ On the third day Abraham looked up and saw the place in the distance.
> ⁵ He said to his servants, "Stay here with the donkey while I and the boy go over there. We will worship and then we will come back to you."
>
> (Genesis 22:1-5)

The fact that God specified the place and the particular mountain for Abraham to sacrifice his son means that the place of sacrifice matters to God. God told him to go to the region of Moriah on a mountain which He (God) was going to tell him. In saying so, God was telling Abraham to be filled with an expectation to hear Him speak. Without this expectation, he would not have heard even when God did speak. Therefore you and I must live daily with a pleasurable anticipation to be directed. Samuel, the boy in the Tabernacle, almost missed the day of his visitation because he was not expecting God would speak to him.

The Bible says, "...*Abraham looked up and saw the place in a distance...* "The only reason he saw the place, though in a distance, is because he lifted up his eyes. Your expectations will cause you to see what others cannot. And once you have seen, it will cause a separation from unnecessary companionship. It will separate you from those who are not relevant for the fulfillment of your destiny.

It is only after Abraham looked up and saw the place of his life-changing destiny-fulfilling sacrifice that he separated himself from his servants. Listen, when you behold that place, you will get separated from anything or anyone who may hinder you or slow you down along that path.

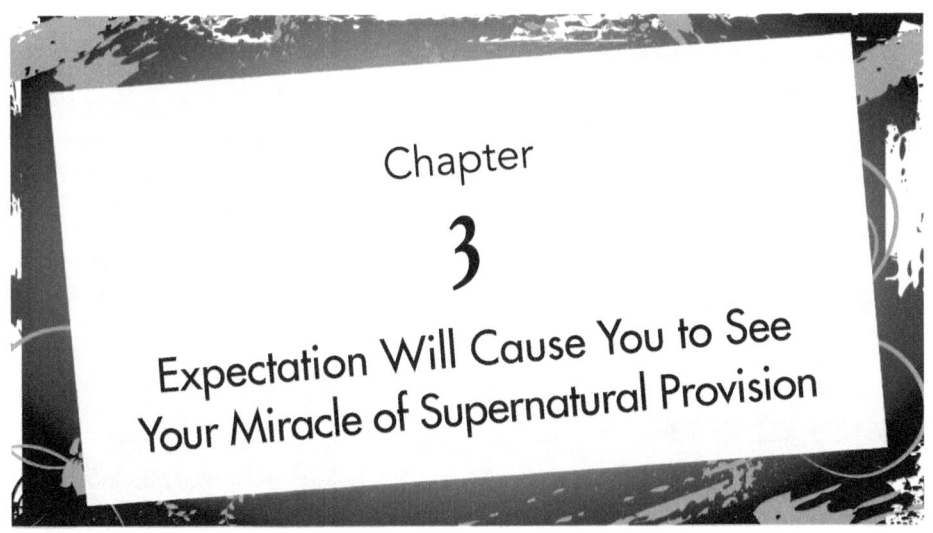

Chapter 3

Expectation Will Cause You to See Your Miracle of Supernatural Provision

Lack of expectation will cause you to be in need longer than you were supposed to. When you cannot lift your eyes beyond your need to the One who is the giver of all good things, you can spend hours, days, months or even years praying for what has already been made available to you. There are many people still searching and asking for what has been searching for them. They are seeking for something that has stood looking at them but they have failed to see because of lack of expectation.

Again about Abraham, the Bible makes it clear that on that mount of sacrifice, when they were on their way,

> "Isaac spoke up and said to his father Abraham, 'Father?'"
> "Yes, my son?" Abraham replied.
> "The fire and wood are here," Isaac said, "but where is the lamb for the burnt offering?"
> 8 Abraham answered, "God himself will provide the lamb for the burnt offering, my son." And the two of them went on together."
>
> Genesis 22:7-8

In order words Abraham was expecting God to provide the Lamb for the sacrifice because He understood that Isaac had been promised to bring forth descendants. And at that moment no descendant of Isaac's had come forth from his loins. That is why verses 13 and 14 of Genesis 22 say, *"13Abraham looked up and there in a thicket he saw a ram caught by its horns. He went over and took the ram and sacrificed it as a burnt offering instead of his son. 14 So Abraham called that place The LORD Will Provide. And to this day it is said, "On the mountain of the LORD it will be provided."* Abraham saw his ram of supernatural provision because he looked up.

When you stop looking down at your lack and you begin looking up at the One who is all sufficient for you, such expectation will open the eyes of your heart to that which God has graciously made available for you. The lamb had been in that place even before Abraham set his feet on that mountain. Abraham's expectation to hear God opened his ears to the voice of God restraining him from killing his son. And it was his expectation to see the miraculous hand of God in providing the lamb that caused him to see what had been made available. You will not stay longer in want than you are supposed to because henceforth, you will be full of the right of expectations.

When Elijah the prophet fled from the city into the wilderness of defeat at the threat of Jezebel, he ran for a long time and become weary and exhausted. Above all he was hungry and depressed. Suddenly he despaired of life and prayed that he might die instead of living. He thought the load was too heavy for him to carry. After praying that he should die, he fell asleep hoping to die in his sleep. I don't know for how long he slept but the Bible says,

> *5 "Then he lay down under the tree and fell asleep. All at once an angel touched him and said, "Get up and eat." 6 He looked around, and there by his head was a cake of bread baked over hot coals, and a jar of water. He ate and drank and then lay down again."*
>
> (I King 19:5-6)

Elijah slept thinking he needed to die meanwhile God knew that a single meal would revive his life and hope. When the angel got him up to eat, the Bible says he *"looked around..."*

In looking around Elijah was releasing his expectations to act in his favor. Until he looked he did not behold the meal God had already provided. Until he looked he did not take note of his miracle. He continued to feel the hunger pangs meanwhile God had provided what he needed.

Even today there are many who are in need of deliverance when God has already made provision for them. So many are in need of blessing because the lack of expectation has caused them to fail to appropriate their *"every spiritual blessing with which God has blessed them in the heavenly realms."* (Ephesians 1:3).

All you need do is lift up your eyes above your circumstances and you will discover your solution has been very close all along. Expectation has power to open someone's eyes to see things in places where others will not see. That is why one man sees only lack of opportunities where another sees a world of possibilities and is faced with the problem of choice. Expectation will open the eyes of your heart. The period of unnecessary want in your life is over because the Holy Spirit will birth in you a holy expectation for the divine supernatural.

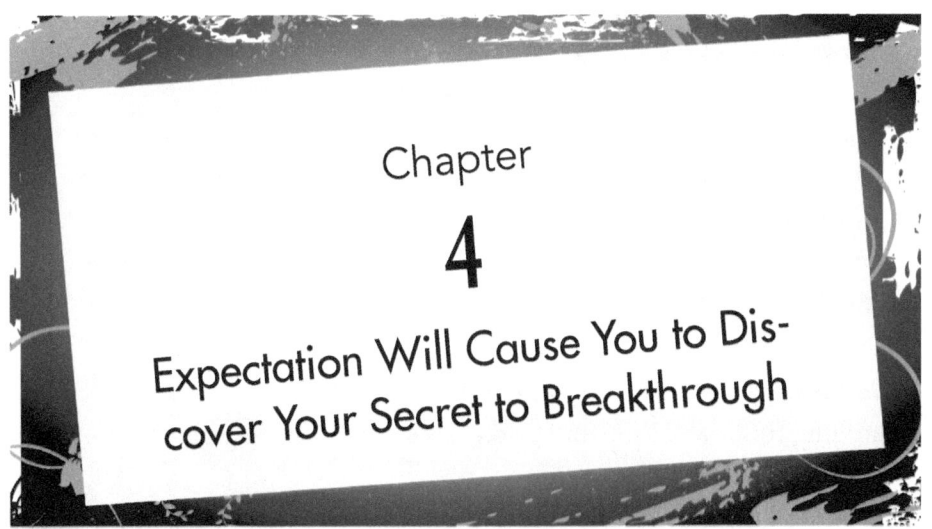

Chapter 4

Expectation Will Cause You to Discover Your Secret to Breakthrough

Many people find themselves before mighty walls of limitation. They find themselves amidst perplexing situations. They are confused and bewildered by the fruitless labor of their lives. They find themselves increasingly cheated by natural circumstances and the greed of fallen humanity. Maybe you have labored night and day, under heat and cold with little to show for it. You find yourself continuously cheated by the changing circumstances around you.

Jacob found himself in such a situation while in the home of Laban, his uncle. In his own words he described his ordeal:

> *38 I have been with you for twenty years now. Your sheep and goats have not miscarried, nor have I eaten rams from your flocks. 39 I did not bring you animals torn by wild beasts; I bore the loss myself. And you demanded payment from me for whatever was stolen by day or night. 40 This was my situation: The heat consumed me in the daytime and the cold at night, and sleep fled from my eyes. 41 It was like this for the twenty years I was in your household. I worked for you fourteen years for your two daughters and six years for your flocks, and you changed my wages ten times. 42 If the God of*

my father, the God of Abraham and the Fear of Isaac, had not been with me, you would surely have sent me away empty-handed. But God has seen my hardship and the toil of my hands, and last night he rebuked you."

(Genesis 31:38-42)

- Are you tired of a life of bearing loss imposed on you by greedy men?
- Are you consumed by heat in the daytime and cold in the night?
- Has sleep fled from your eyes, you lay down but cannot sleep?

Have the circumstances surrounding you left you empty-handed with little or nothing to show in spite of all your hard work, and toilsome labour?

That was exactly the case with Jacob until something happened. Expectation has power! The power of expectation brought about a breakthrough for Jacob. He recounted the secret of his breakthrough to his wives when he explained

10 "In breeding season I once had a dream in which I looked up and saw that the male goats mating with the flock were streaked, speckled or spotted. 11 The angel of God said to me in the dream, `Jacob.' I answered, `Here I am.' 12 And he said, `Look up and see that all the male goats mating with the flock are streaked, speckled or spotted, for I have seen all that Laban has been doing to you. 13 I am the God of Bethel, where you anointed a pillar and where you made a vow to me. Now leave this land at once and go back to your native land.'"

(Genesis 31:10-13).

What did the angel tell Jacob? He said *"Look up and see…"* Jacob had to look up before he could see. He had to look up i.e. be filled with expectation so as to take note of what brought him breakthrough. Expectation will give you undiscovered ideas that will bring about unprecedented breakthrough in your business or vocation. Expectation demonstrates to God that you are not contented with being a failure in business or in ministry. Expectation triggers a release and an impartation of divine ideas. The Lord told Jeremiah to *"call unto me, and I will answer thee, and show thee great and mighty things thou knowest not".* (Jer. 33:3 KJV).

Your expectation for breakthrough will orchestrate your desperate calling. And your calling will meet with a response accompanied by revelation of secrets from the throne. The NIV of that verse is: *"call to me and I will answer you and tell you great and unsearchable things you do not know."*

We are talking about ideas beyond human comprehension.

We are talking about ideas that still lie hidden to science or other people in the same business as you. That is what expectation will do for you. It will orchestrate breakthrough for you as it did for Jacob. By applying what he received from God and by looking up to Him for breakthrough, the Bible says Jacob *"grew exceedingly prosperous and came to own large flocks, and maid servants and menservants, and camels and donkeys."* (Gen 30:43). I feel like jumping! Do you see that description? He became exceedingly prosperous! A single idea and you move twenty years ahead of your peers.

Henceforth your peers will no longer measure up to you. Your night of toil and hardship is over. You will no longer complain, murmur or grumble. Your life will be one of laughter and delight because of the breakthrough that is coming your way. For the Holy Spirit will birth in you a holy expectation for breakthrough. I see you coming out of lack into plenty. I see your story changing in the split of a second because of a divinely imparted idea.

Expectation has power to orchestrate breakthrough!

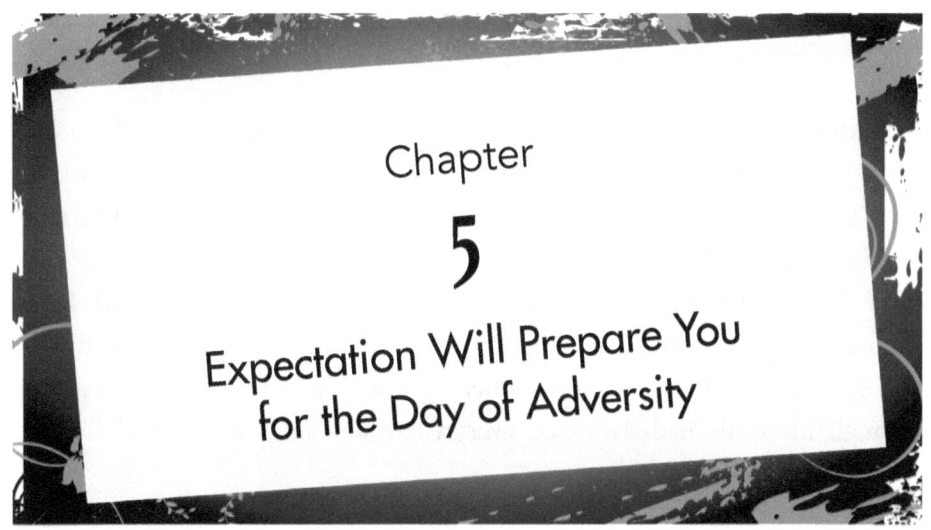

Chapter 5
Expectation Will Prepare You for the Day of Adversity

Lately, I came to discover that there is a day of trouble for everyone. It is just a matter of time. Certainly each one has his day of trouble. The Lord told the Psalmist *"And call upon Me in the day of trouble; I will deliver you, and you will honor Me"* (Ps 50:15). So you see that there is a day of trouble for each one of us. You must be ready and prepared for the day of trouble. Expectation is what makes you prepared to face all forms of adversity. The one full of expectation is ready to call and receive response.

Job, in the midst of his fiery ordeals, when his whole world crumbled around him, when he lost everything what kept him going was his expectation.

He said "Though he slay me, yet will I hope in Him" (Job 13:15a). This implies no matter what was happening, Job decided to expect good things from the Lord. He kept his expectation in God. By so doing he could brave it through all kinds of trial or difficulty he encountered. Hope is the quality by which faith is demonstrated. Without hope faith has no way to express itself.

Again, listen to what Job said in order to understand the power that is stored up in expectation: *"I know that my Redeemer lives, and that in the end he will stand upon the earth. And after my skin has been destroyed, yet in my flesh I will see God; I myself will see him with my own eyes—I, and not another. How my heart yearns within me!"* (Job 19:25-27).

Job's knowledge that his Redeemer is alive kept him going through the storm. In fact he had the expectation to see his Redeemer in his flesh and with his own eyes. Because of this expectation his heart yearned within him. Anyone full of the right kind of expectation will make it through the most fiery trials that life can offer. But the lack of expectation will cause a breakdown in the most trivial of problems. Though Job's flesh was at this time wasted, he still expected God's intervention. I believe that is why his flesh was restored. Though his trials had darkened everywhere around him, he still had his expectation to see God.

You can only go as far as your expectations and you can only rise as far as your expectations will take you.

When Jacob was returning from Aram to Canaan, he knew that adversity was waiting for him. This is because his records were not clean when he left Canaan for Aram. However, *"Jacob looked up and there was Esau, coming with his four hundred men; so he divided the children among Leah, Rachel and the two maidservants. ² He put the maidservants and their children in front, Leah and her children next, and Rachel and Joseph in the rear. ³ He himself went on ahead and bowed down to the ground seven times as he approached his brother."* (Gen 33:1-3). Because of his expectation, he made adequate preparation. He *"looked up and…"* saw trouble coming from afar. Had he been void of expectation he wouldn't have looked up and trouble would have fallen on him unprepared.

Expectation will cause you to anticipate pitfalls and guard against them. Expectation will cause you to discover the traps and snares of the enemy and jump over. Because of lack of expectations many have fallen and are caught in very obvious traps of the enemy. May it not happen to you! As you look up may the Lord open your eyes to behold the wiles of the enemy and provide a safe escape for you. There is revelation power in expectation.

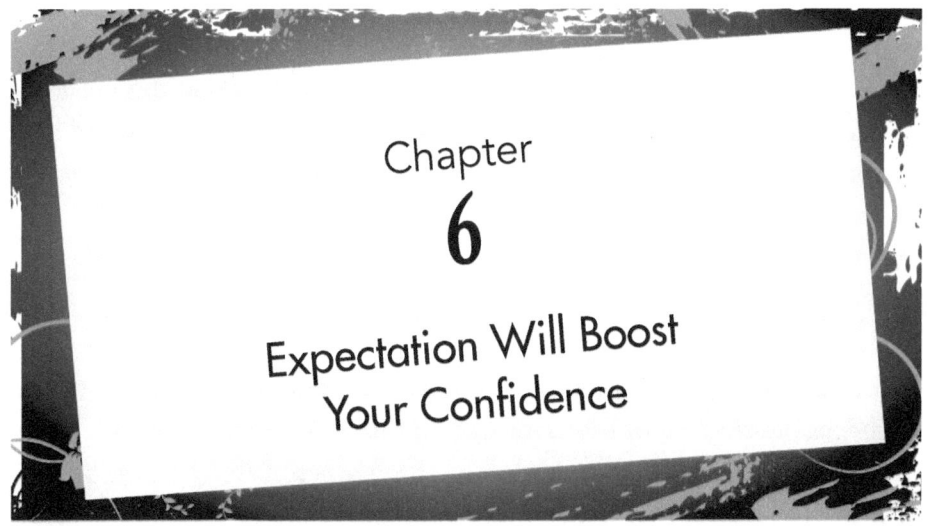

Chapter 6

Expectation Will Boost Your Confidence

The Christian life is one of warfare. It is a life in which the Christian is called to live not for himself any longer but for the One who gave His all to redeem him from the tyranny of sin. There are many enormous challenges to be faced along the path to heaven. The Christian constantly needs to demonstrate a confident disposition against his adversaries. When this happens victory is easy to maintain.

Just today I spent quite some time trying to get someone confident in her faith. She is a former marine agent of darkness whom I delivered. Recently she has come under attack and she seemed to be panic-stricken. I told her as long as she allows fear to get hold of her, demons and other agents will keep attacking her until she begins to demonstrate her confidence in the power of Jesus.

Expectation, i.e. lifting up one's eyes to Jesus is a sure boost to one's confidence. As long as you look at the raging waves, torrential storms, or flood waters, your confidence will diminish. Looking up to Jesus lifts your confidence to a higher cadence, evident to all your obstacles. When Israel got into the Promise Land they were faced with the great challenge of Jericho. The Bible says, *"Now when Joshua was near Jericho, he looked up and saw a man standing in front of him with a drawn sword in his hand. Joshua went up to him and asked, "Are you for us or for our enemies?"* (Jos 5:13).

Between Joshua and the full inheritance of the Israelites stood this great obstacle, Jericho. I am quite sure seeing the Jericho wall, Joshua wondered how he could ever scale it, let alone push it down so as to win this determinant battle. Why did Joshua look up? Because he came to a fast conclusion that the obstacle before him was greater than any other he had encountered either under Moses or since he became commander of the army.

In lifting up his eyes he was turning totally to another source for strength and confidence in the face of this challenge. In lifting up his eyes and beholding the Lord Jesus, he now saw this obstacle through Jesus. And because he now saw these mighty walls of Jericho through Jesus who is greater and mightier, his confidence was boosted. He no longer saw it as impossibility.

My dear friend, between you and that wall of Jericho which has stood on your way is Jesus Christ, Lord of lords and King of kings. If you will just lift up your eyes from yourself and look at Him in earnest expectation your confidence to face life's challenges will receive an unprecedented boost. And the boost in confidence will cause the odds to diminish. One vital secret in life is to measure every obstacle through the Lord Jesus Christ. Expectation will cause you to see everything through the eyes of Jesus.

The Psalmist said, *"Be strong and take heart, all you who hope in the LORD"* (Ps 31:24).

In other words strength and confidence will come to all those who have placed their expectations in the Lord. Do you want to be strong and confident always? Then place all your expectations in the Lord and in no-one or nothing else. When you do this all else may fail, everyone may desert, disappoint and even despise you but nothing will be able to shake or diminish your confidence to face every mountain, sea or gulf that stands on your way. Confidence in the Lord will provide you wings when needed.

It will form a bridge when needed and act as a lift when appropriate. So lift up those eyes and look to Jesus. There is tremendous power is expectation to boost your confidence.

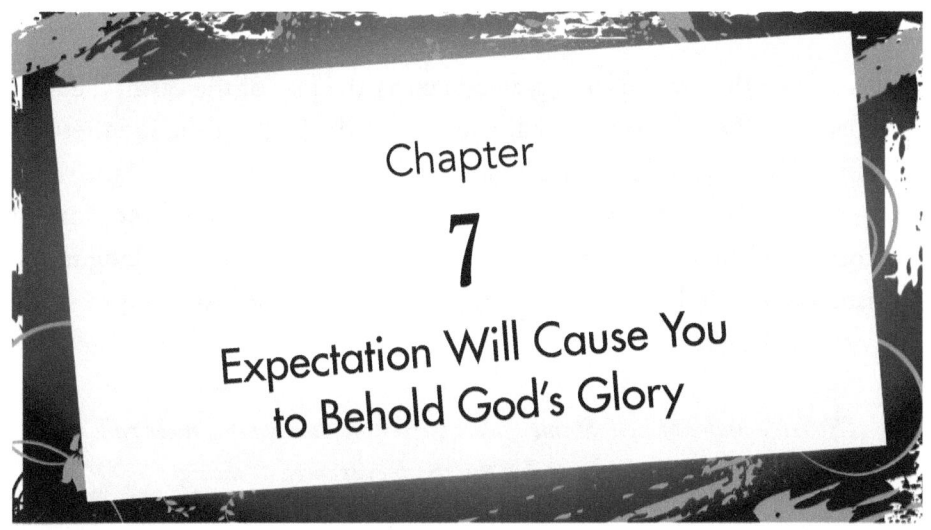

Chapter 7
Expectation Will Cause You to Behold God's Glory

Many people fail to see the glory of God in the beauty of nature and in the things surrounding them because of lack of expectation. Lack of expectation is what is causing many to take a gloomy disposition to life. Listen, if you are filled with the right kind of expectation, you can behold God's glory through the thickest clouds.

Expectation will cause you to see His glory in the storms and flames that come your way. A man who constantly beholds the glory of the Creator in everything remains a marvel to the forces of evil. In the face of the fieriest ordeal, such a person can laugh. And such holy laughter tantalizes the enemy.

Now the Ark of the Covenant had been captured in battle by the Philistines. And since the Ark represented the glory, the Israelites said the glory had departed from the nation. Throughout the stay of the Ark in Philistia untold havoc was wrought by the Lord in their midst. Life in Israel had not returned to normal because the ark was not, and therefore, the glory was absent. In spite of this, they were still a people who decided to look beyond the immediate so as to behold the glory returning to the nation. They lifted up their eyes above the business of the day. They looked beyond their harvest to behold the glory returning.

I tell you that though darkness seems to cover the face of the earth, the man of expectation can see beyond that and behold the glory of the soon returning King. Those who behold such glory cannot help but rejoice at the sight. As the Spirit of God fills you with expectation and you behold the glory of the coming of the Lord, yours will become a joyful life. Joy is lacking in the Christian milieu today because the abundant harvest instead seems to shade our view of the glory.

> *"Now the people of Beth Shemesh were harvesting their wheat in the valley, and when they looked up and saw the ark, they rejoiced at the sight."*
>
> (1Sa 6:13)

Though the people of Beth Shemesh were harvesting, there was no joy until they saw the ark returning. What gives the Christian joy is not actually the harvest but the glory of the King. It is the manifestation of the returning glory that enlivens and invigorates the believer. And expectation is what will cause you to behold the glory.

What about Stephen? In face of his trials, he lifted up his eyes beyond his persecutors and saw the glory of God.

> *55 "But Stephen, full of the Holy Spirit, looked up to heaven and saw the glory of God, and Jesus standing at the right hand of God. 56 "Look," he said, "I see heaven open and the Son of Man standing at the right hand of God."*
>
> (Acts 7:55-56)

One filled with expectation can confidently face life's trials. He can stand in front of the most intimidating crowd and defend the gospel. There is power in expectation to cause you to behold the glory of God. And when you have beheld that glory nothing becomes too dear for you to lay down, not even your life.

After a man has beheld the glory he can still pray for forgiveness even for someone who is killing him. Expectation tears the veil of blindness and exposes the eyes of your inner man to the glory of the King. When Paul wrote, *"But whenever anyone turns to the Lord, the veil is taken away"* (2 Co 3:16), he understood that turning to the Lord is a manifestation of expectation that He can do something. When you demonstrate such expectation the Lord then takes away anything that distorts your view of His life transforming glory.

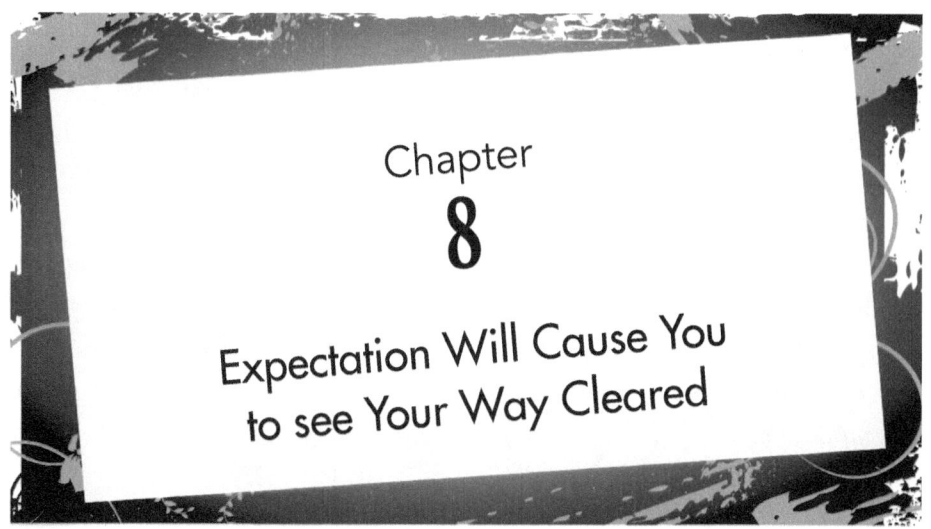

Chapter 8

Expectation Will Cause You to see Your Way Cleared

Each day comes with several open doors and several opportunities for you to move towards your God-ordained destiny. Expectation will not only cause you to see these open doors but will lead you to choose rightly. There are many people standing before open doors but they fail to perceive them because of the lack of expectation. They have failed to lift up their eyes beyond the difficulties that apparently stand on their way.

The truth is that many of our difficulties are only fears. Most of what we consider to be great obstacles are only imaginary. These fears and imaginations take root from past knowledge and past experiences. That is why it is very dangerous for anyone to live in the past. The past shades and obstruct one's view of the present. The past has the capacity to inspire fear by causing false evidences to appear real.

After the crucifixion and death of our Savior and Lord Jesus Christ, the Bible says, "*46 So Joseph bought some linen cloth, took down the body, wrapped it in the linen, and placed it in a tomb cut out of rock. Then he rolled a stone against the entrance of the tomb. 47 Mary Magdalene and Mary the mother of Joses saw where he was laid.*" (Mk 15:46-47).

These women were eye witnesses to the mighty stone being put at the mouth of the grave and so they went home with that knowledge. For three whole days they lived with the knowledge of this impossible barrier that had been placed at the mouth of the tomb, stopping access into the tomb by whosoever. Each night these women went to bed, and got up each morning with the knowledge that the stone was at the mouth of the grave.

Again, it is written *"¹ When the Sabbath was over, Mary Magdalene, Mary the mother of James, and Salome bought spices so that they might go to anoint Jesus' body. ² Very early on the first day of the week, just after sunrise, they were on their way to the tomb ³ and they asked each other, "Who will roll the stone away from the entrance of the tomb?" ⁴ But when they looked up, they saw that the stone, which was very large, had been rolled away."* (Mk 16:1-4)

These women had a picture in their mind of what no longer existed. They talked, murmured and complained to each other about an obstacle which was no longer present. This would have caused them to miss being witnesses of the resurrection because they dwelt on false evidence that still appeared real.

And there are many people who see impossibilities where there are none because they bring their past knowledge into the present even though it is not applicable. There are many people who have stopped on the pathway to great discoveries because of imaginary obstacles. Some waste several calories complaining of, and murmuring about non-existent things.

All this is because of one thing—the lack of expectation. As long as anyone concentrates on the problem, expectation is lacking. Their question, *"who will roll the stone away…"* was baseless because at this time, there was no stone at the entrance. It was a question birthed from ignorance. And there are countless people today who are asking ignorant questions. They make ignorant complains and plan strategies birthed out of ignorance of what God has already accomplished on their behalf. You must learn to be current with the move of the Spirit.

"But when _they looked up_, they saw that the stone, which was very large, had been rolled away." Do not let your conception of the size of the obstacle hinder you from seeing what God has already accomplished on your behalf. Until these women looked up, they never saw that their obstacle was no longer there.

May you too look up and see that the way has been cleared for you. Expectation births pleasant surprises and takes you through the unimaginable. Expectation has power to deliver from complaining and murmuring. It opens your eyes to the great things God has done for you.

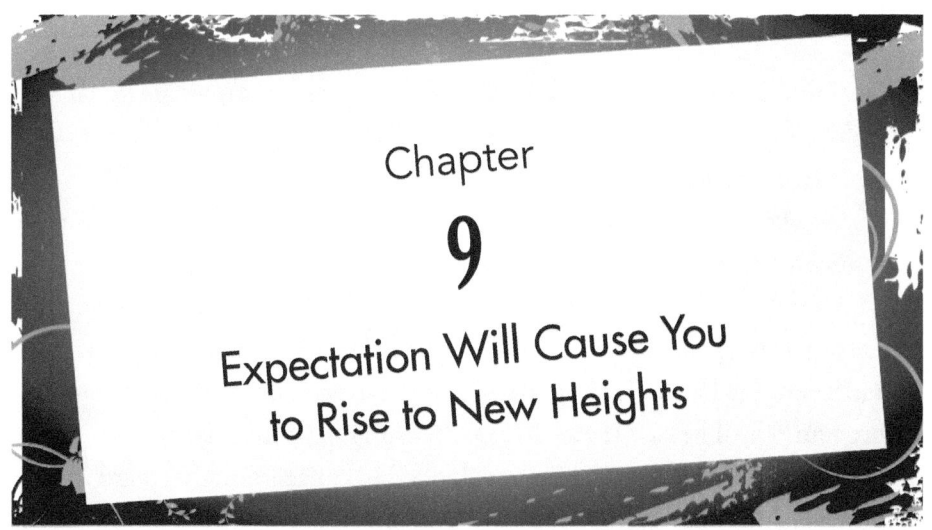

Chapter 9
Expectation Will Cause You to Rise to New Heights

Like I said in the previous section, many of us stand before God-ordained open doors yet fail to perceive them and therefore we cease to make the progress we are supposed to. Many people spend time praying for open doors meanwhile they fail to see and make use of their already-provided open doors.

The Lord Jesus is saying to each one of us, *"See, I have placed before you an open door that no one can shut."* (Rev 3:8b). Now in order for you to see your open door you have to look, that is to say you must have an expectation. The open door is already there and no one can shut it, but you must see it in order for you to go through it. This reminds me of a friend who stood in front of a door calling for a brother to come with the keys meanwhile the door was not even locked. He stood there for quite some time until the other brother came and told him the door was not locked. His ignorance of the fact that the door was not locked caused him to waste time outside in the cold meanwhile he would have gone in and slept.

There are many of you standing before open doors that just need to be shaken a bit and the way will open wide before you. May you not stay there longer than you are supposed to because of ignorance. There is an open door before you. You must look in order to see it.

About John, it is written, *"¹After this I looked, and there before me was a door standing open in heaven. And the voice I had first heard speaking to me like a trumpet said, "Come up here, and I will show you what must take place after this." ² At once I was in the Spirit, and there before me was a throne in heaven with someone sitting on it."* (Rev 4:1-2)

There was this open door John had before him but which he had not seen or perceived. He had to look in order to see the open door that was standing before him. Until he saw the open door nothing happened. But immediately he saw this open door because he now looked in expectation, he heard a voice say to him, *"come up here…"*

The command to come up was only given because John now saw the open door. God wants you to rise beyond where you are.

If you perceive that open door, you shall hear the command to rise to new heights.

God is saying to you:

> *"Come up here into My joy from your sorrow"*
> *"Come up here, out of your poverty into My riches".*
> *"Come up here, out of your sickness into My health"*
> *"Come up here, out of your distress into My rest"*
> *"Come up here, from mediocrity into excellence".*
> *"Come up here, out of your defeat into My victory".*
> *"Come up here, out of your bondage into My freedom".*
> *"Come up here, out of your disillusionment into My hope".*

You need not stay longer in that miserable situation. You must rise up from your present level to where God is taking you. When you see your open door, there is just one direction for you. And that is upward! When John went up

He appeared before the throne. Like him your expectation will cause you to rise to untold heights to the place of authority. May the Spirit of the Living God birth in you expectation so that you will be propelled to your God-ordained heights.

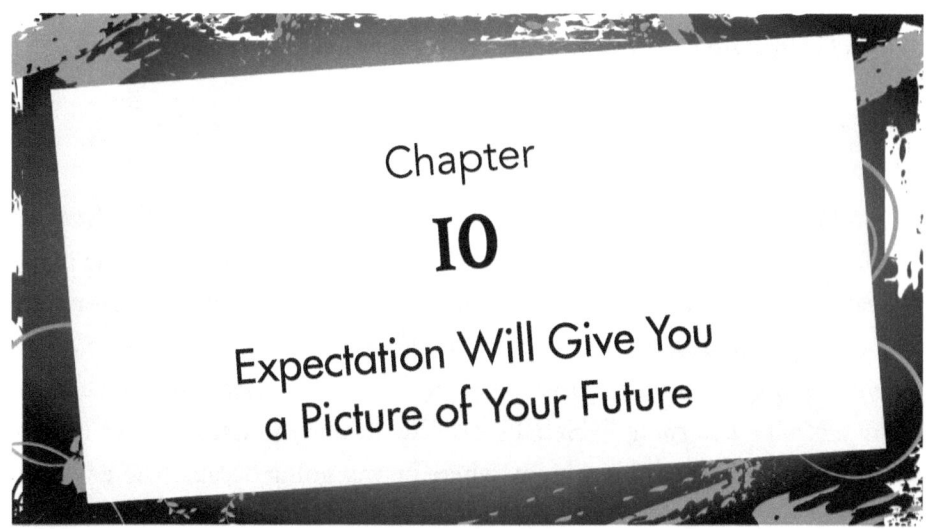

Chapter 10
Expectation Will Give You a Picture of Your Future

Expectation has the capacity to open up the future, at least part of it. In the previous section, John's expectation caused him to be shown what was going to happen. The Lord told Israel, through the Prophet Jeremiah, *"For I know the thoughts that I think towards you, to give you an expected end"* (Jer 29:11 KJV).

Therefore what will take you into the future God has for you is expectation. And for expectation to take you there it gives you a picture of where you are going to. God has prepared a great future for you but unless your heart becomes filled with expectations of what He has in store for your future, everything will remain hidden. But as you anticipate with pleasure to get there, the Spirit of God will birth mental pictures of what He has in store for you.

When God had called Abraham and separated him from his nation, people, tribe, and family. He told him:

> *"¹ Leave your country, your people and your father's household and go to the land I will show you.*

> "²*I will make you into a great nation and I will bless you; I will make your name great, and you will be a blessing.*³ *I will bless those who bless you, and whoever curses you I will curse; and all peoples on earth will be blessed through you.*"
>
> (Gen 12:1-3).

When God said this, the Bible says, "*So Abraham left, as the LORD had told him...* " (v 4). However Abraham had no picture of what it meant being made a great nation. Neither did he understand what it meant having a great name. The writer of Hebrew writes: "*By faith Abraham, when called to go to a place he would later receive as his inheritance, obeyed and went, even though he did not know where he was going.*" (Heb 11:8). This means though he never understood he obeyed. He did not know where he was going because there was no picture of his future. However the LORD knew that Abraham needed a picture of his future, at least just a glimpse of what had been prepared for him. So in chapter fifteen of Genesis, the Lord decided to give him a motivational picture of His great plans for Abraham.

> "⁵ *He took him outside and said, "Look up at the heavens and count the stars--if indeed you can count them." Then he said to him, "So shall your offspring be."*
> ⁶ *Abram believed the LORD, and he credited it to him as righteousness.*"
>
> (Gen 15:5-6)

The preceding verses give a detailed discussion between the Lord and Abraham. Though Abraham had obeyed the call to separation he did not fully understand the detail of the promise and so he complained to God about someone else becoming his heir. What accounted for this was Abraham's lack of expectation of a child and so there was no ground on which his faith could act. Faith demonstrates itself on one's expectation.

For God to trigger Abraham's faith, he had to take him out of his tent into the darkness. This is because while in his tent Abraham could only see as far as the roof of the tent. So the Lord brought him to a place where he could have a clear mental understanding of what was in store for him. When he came out, He told him *"Look up…"* These were the first words in that conversation to motivate Abraham to be filled with expectation, to hope beyond what he had seen in the natural. God understood that as Abraham looked down at himself he could not rise above his problems. So He was telling Abraham to have a different focus – the heavens, where God's throne is. So in looking up to the heavens and seeing its vastness, beauty, the brightness and number of the stars, Abraham was given a picture of his great future. When he received this picture of his future, he believed the LORD.

Henceforth you shall not doubt God! The Spirit of God will birth in you an expectation that will give you a mental picture of your future. And this will cause you to believe everything the Lord has told you in His Book. Many people doubt because they lack this expectation which should give them a glimpse of their God ordained future.

There is power in expectation to open a window to the future God has planned for you.

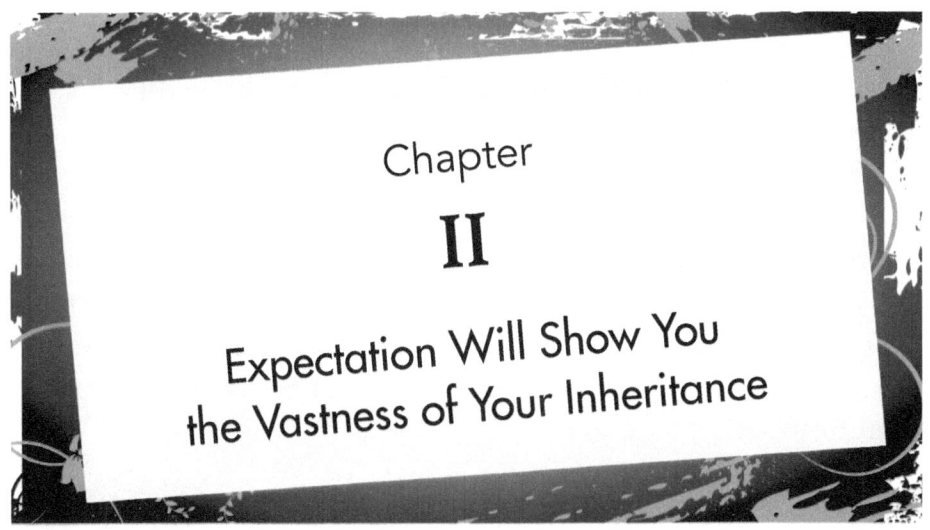

Chapter II
Expectation Will Show You the Vastness of Your Inheritance

"However, as it is written:
"No eye has seen, no ear has heard, no mind has conceived what God has prepared for those who love him"-- but God has revealed it to us by his Spirit. The Spirit searches all things, even the deep things of God."

(I Co 2:9-10)

Naturally you never develop any mental picture of what God has accomplished on your behalf. Your natural eyes cannot see all of it even if it was shown you in the natural. Your natural mind can never conceive the vastness of your heritage in Christ Jesus. It is only the Holy Spirit who can reveal it to you. And He does so by filling you with expectation. It is expectation that provides the atmosphere for further revelation.

Many of us have not understood the vastness of what Christ accomplished for us. In fact it is so vast that even a lifetime will not be enough to appropriate all of it. Nevertheless you cannot receive more than what you appropriate and you cannot appropriate what you have not seen spiritually. And you cannot see what has not been revealed to you. Again we see the indispensable need for expectation to be born in your heart. That is what the Holy Spirit will use to show you how vast your inheritance is and how much of it you still have to possess.

After Lot had chosen the best part of the land (so he thought) for himself, Abraham was left wondering what was left for him. That is when God spoke to him after he had left his nation, people, and family: *"The LORD said to Abram after Lot had parted from him, "Lift up your eyes from where you are and look north and south, east and west. ¹⁵ All the land that you see I will give to you and your offspring forever. ¹⁶ I will make your offspring like the dust of the earth, so that if anyone could count the dust, then your offspring could be counted. ¹⁷ Go, walk through the length and breadth of the land, for I am giving it to you."* (Gen 13:14 – 17).

Again here you see the command for Abraham to lift up his eyes. O, The tremendous power that is released through expectation! My friend, expectation will take your eyes off the evil men have done to you. It will take your eyes off where you have failed and messed things up. It will take your eyes from your lack into the vastness of what God through Christ Jesus has accomplished for you.

Expectation will lift your eyes from every loss onto the vastness of your inheritance. Expectation will keep you from fighting with those who have cheated you. Abraham could only see the vastness of his inheritance after he lifted up his eyes. Without lifting up his eyes he could not behold the vastness of what God has given him. After he beheld the vastness of his inheritance God told him to appropriate it through a prayer walk.

Listen, expectation will not only reveal to you the vastness of your inheritance but will show you what prophetic actions to take in order to appropriate what has been given you. May you be filled with expectation from this very moment!

The Psalmist said, *"LORD, you have assigned me my portion and my cup; you have made my lot secure. The boundary lines have fallen for me in pleasant places; surely I have a delightful inheritance."* (Ps 16:5-6)

God has assigned you your portion and your cup. And it is a fat portion; it is a cup full and running over. He has made your lot secure. And indeed the boundary lines have fallen for you in pleasant places. Your inheritance is a delightful one.

However, until you see these with the eyes of your heart you cannot begin appropriating any of it. Seeing is prerequisite to appropriating. And appropriating is prerequisite to enjoying. May your expectation bring you to begin enjoying all God has accomplished for you in Christ Jesus in every domain of the human life!

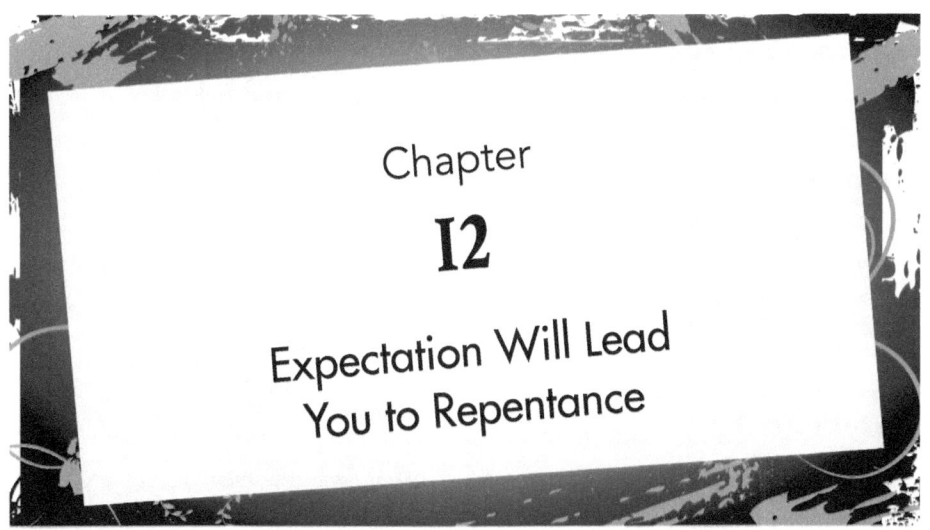

Chapter 12

Expectation Will Lead You to Repentance

Many people come to the place where they find it difficult to repent because of lack of expectation. One filled with expectation keeps short records with sin and ensures that there is nothing to hinder his receiving the object of his expectation.

Sin, whether by commission or omission, can cut off one's expectation if not properly dealt with. Proverbs 10:28 says, *"The hope of the righteous shall be gladness: but the expectation of the wicked shall perish."* (KJV) Thus sin has the capacity to kill a man's expectation. There are people who once were full of Holy Ghost-inspired expectations but because they indulged into sin, those expectations perished. May yours not perish, in Jesus' Name.

On the other hand the Bible admonishes, *"Let not thine heart envy sinners: but be thou in the fear of the LORD all the day long. For surely there is an end; and thine expectation shall not be cut off."* (Pr 23:17-18, KJV). The fear of the Lord, holiness and righteousness are what sustain a man's hopes and dreams. You have a guaranteed expectation when you live holy because nothing will be able to cut it off.

Anybody without the right expectation will indulge in sin and compromise. It is your expectation that will cause you to rise when you fall. Some have fallen and indulged in their mud of sin because they thought all their hope was gone. Listen, true expectation does not vanish that quickly.

When the first set of captives had returned to the land of Canaan, from their captivity in Babylon, some men got themselves entangled in the sin of intermarriage with the people of the land. This had been clearly forbidden by the law. When the sin was realized by Ezra, leader of these returning exiles, the Bible says,

> *"¹ While Ezra was praying and confessing, weeping and throwing himself down before the house of God, a large crowd of Israelites--men, women and children--gathered around him. They too wept bitterly. ² Then Shecaniah son of Jehiel, one of the descendants of Elam, said to Ezra, "We have been unfaithful to our God by marrying foreign women from the peoples around us. But in spite of this, there is still hope for Israel.³ Now let us make a covenant before our God to send away all these women and their children, in accordance with the counsel of my lord and of those who fear the commands of our God. Let it be done according to the Law. ⁴ Rise up; this matter is in your hands. We will support you, so take courage and do it."*
>
> (Ezra 10:1-4).

Ezra wept and wailed because of the gravity of the offense at hand. He prayed and confessed the sins of the people because he expected God to forgive them.

My focus here is verse 2. Listen, in spite of how far you have fallen, in spite of how soiled you are, the slightest hope will push you to repent and make proper amends. Ezra rose up and gathered courage to deal with the situation because there was still hope for Israel. Some of you have given up already, thinking that all hope for forgiveness is gone because of the sin you committed.

The fact that you even feel the slightest guilt for your sin shows that there is still hope for you. And because there is still hope, you need not give up. You need not continue in that state of compromise and indulgence. God will forgive you and cleanse you if you will repent. There is still hope for you! Rise up from that fallen position. Walk out of that indulgence. Separate yourself unto the Lord. No matter how painful it may take to put things right, do not hesitate to do it. God is still patient with you. Expectation has power to push a man to true repentance.

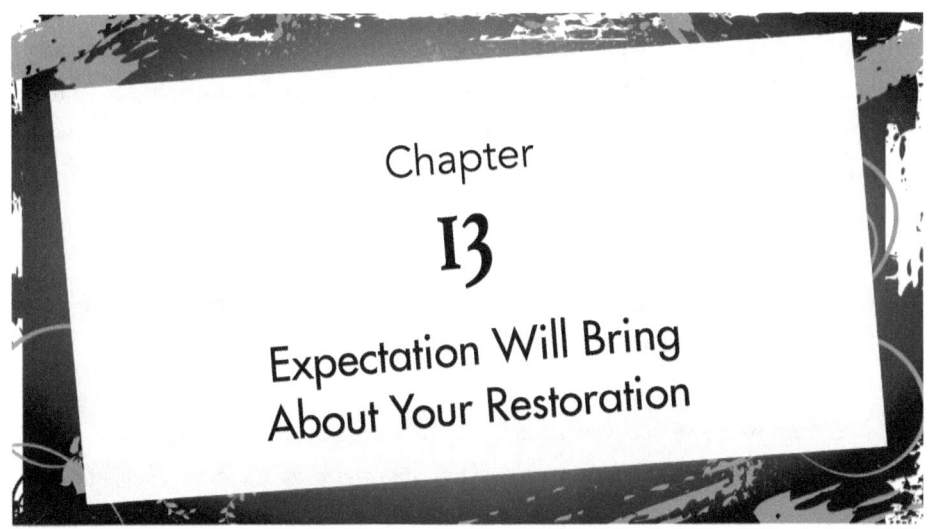

Chapter

13

Expectation Will Bring About Your Restoration

"Lift up your eyes and look around; all your sons gather and come to you. As surely as I live," declares the LORD, "you will wear them all as ornaments; you will put them on, like a bride. Though you were ruined and made desolate and your land laid waste, now you will be too small for your people, and those who devoured you will be far away."

(Isa 49:18-19)

No matter the calamity which has befallen you, no matter the extent to which the storms of life have stripped you of your blessings and possessions, if you do not allow the storms of life to cut off your hope then a double restoration is your guaranteed portion when the storms are over. The Lord told Israel to lift up her eyes and look. This was a call to be filled with expectation of a total, complete, and permanent restoration. The capacity to see a bright future through the darkness of the storms is that which expectation births in a man. And when you hold on to this picture of a bright future, restoration is bound to come.

Restoration is not automatic after the storms of life. Your degree of expectation will determine your degree of restoration of what has been lost in the storms. Where this expectation for restoration is lacking, you will continue to feel and suffer the effects of the storm even after it is long ended. That is why you can see two people who have gone through the same kind of trouble but one has been healed from the scars and has received complete restoration while the other is still growling in the aftermath. The simple reason for the complex difference in the situations is the presence of great expectations in one life and the absence of it in the other.

Now, read these words and meditate on them in order for you to see the power of expectation to bring you restoration:

> *"Lift up your eyes and look about you: All assemble and come to you; your sons come from afar, and your daughters are carried on the arm. Then you will look and be radiant, your heart will throb and swell with joy; the wealth on the seas will be brought to you, to you the riches of the nations will come. Herds of camels will cover your land, young camels of Midian and Ephah. And all from Sheba will come, bearing gold and incense and proclaiming the praise of the LORD. All Kedar's flocks will be gathered to you, the rams of Nebaioth will serve you; they will be accepted as offerings on my altar, and I will adorn my glorious temple."*
>
> (Isa 60:4-7).

The rest of the promises of restoration found in these verses are tied to the simple command to lift up your eyes and look.

- ➢ Expectation will restore your family life!
- ➢ Expectation will restore God's radiant glory in your life!
- ➢ Expectation will restore you to a joyful life!
- ➢ Expectation will restore you and bring you wealth!

There is tremendous power for restoration released from an expectant heart.

No matter the prison or dungeon in which you find yourself, if you have not lost hope, then a double restoration will come to you. The LORD is saying to you, *"Return to your fortress, O prisoners of hope; even now I announce that I will restore twice as much to you"* (Zec 9:12).

You may be in prison but as long as you still have hope you open the way for your restoration. Hope or expectation provides the rails on which your train of restoration will move. At the same time, it is the fuel for your train of restoration. So when it is lacking your restoration train is without fuel to propel it or rails for it to move on.

We said in the previous section that expectation will lead you to repentance. And you know that restoration can only come after heart-rending and true repentance. Do you now see how indispensable it is to be a man, woman, boy or girl of hope?

There is power in expectation to bring you restoration!

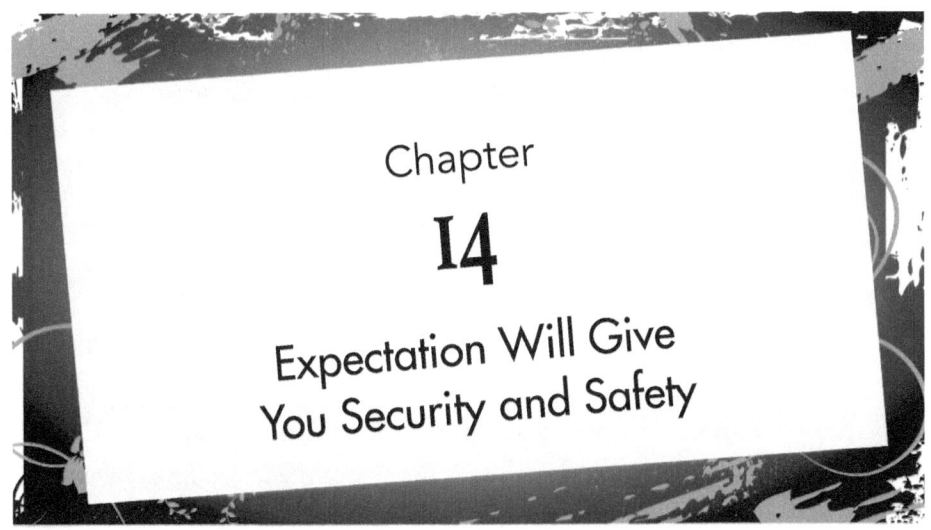

Chapter 14
Expectation Will Give You Security and Safety

There are many people, even professing Christians who live in constant insecurity, even when there is no need for alarm. They may be rich or poor, young or old, trained or untrained, educated or uneducated. This is because what brings security is not money, neither is it a job, nor a home nor education nor age.

In fact, it can even be said that the richer a man, the more insecure he is. The more educated the more insecure. That is why you find some of them doing several PhD's, all because of insecurity in life. There is just one thing that brings lasting and wholesome security, and that is hope. Where there is no hope, doubt, fear of the future, panic and all kinds of instability creep in and so does insecurity.

Show me an insecure man or woman, boy or girl, and then you have indirectly shown me one without hope. Hope is what births inner strength and unfeigned confidence in you. And it is inner strength and confidence that keep away insecurity.

"Yet if you devote your heart to him and stretch out your hands to him, if you put away the sin that is in your hand and allow no evil to dwell in your tent, then you will lift up your face without shame; you will stand firm and without fear. You will surely forget your trouble, recalling it only as waters gone by. Life will be brighter than noonday, and darkness will become like morning. You will be secure, because there is hope; you will look about you and take your rest in safety. You will lie down, with no one to make you afraid, and many will court your favor. But the eyes of the wicked will fail, and escape will elude them; their hope will become a dying gasp."

(Job 11:13-20)

We already mentioned the fact that sin cuts off one's expectation as reiterated by verses 13-14. You must deal with the sin in your life if you must have hope restored to you. Look at verse 15; "You will lift up your face…"

This is hope! This is expectation!

Many people are insecure because of shame but expectation will drive away your shame!

- Expectation will cause you to stand firm!
- Expectation will cause you to live without fear!
- Expectation will cause you to forget your trouble!
- Expectation will make you to be secure!
- Expectation will cause you to rest in safety!
- Expectation will bring radiance and brightness into your life!
- Expectation will convert your darkness into morning!
- Expectation will cause you to live and sleep with all confidence!
- Expectation will make you bold, afraid of nothing!
- Expectation will make men and women want to identify with you!

At noonday, shadows are minimal. So if your life becomes as bright as noonday, anything that shades vision will be taken away from you! It means all that blocks the rays of the light of revelation will be dispelled.

Expectation Will Give You Security and Safety

I see every trace of insecurity going far from you because of the expectation being birthed in you now!

- I see your fears fleeing!
- I see your shadows disappearing!
- I see your shame losing its hold on you!
- I see you forgetting your former troubles!
- I see men seeking your favour because your blessing and prosperity will be evident!
- I see you laughing at your trails and singing in your storms!
- I see you entering into total and wholesome spiritual rest!
- There is power in expectation!

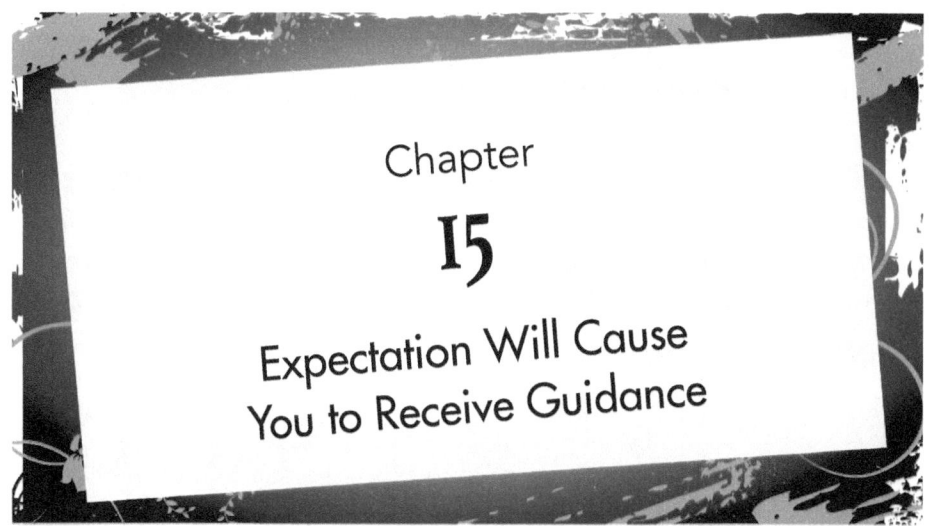

Chapter 15

Expectation Will Cause You to Receive Guidance

As children of God we constantly need God's guidance in our daily life, and He has promised to guide us. He says: *"I will instruct thee and teach thee in the way which thou shalt go: I will guide thee with Mine eye"* (Ps 32:8). Elsewhere it is written, *"The LORD will guide you always"* (Isa 58:11). However in order to benefit from such guidance we must live daily expecting to be guided. It is your expectation that will cause you to benefit from God's continuous guidance.

According to Dr. Westley Duewel, in *"Let God Guide You Daily"*,

> *"Guidance is to be one of the marks that distinguish you as a child of God", because "those who are led by the Spirit of God are sons of God" (Rom 8:14). God wants you to have joyful assurance that He is leading you into your future. By this He adds direction and significance to your life. Are you eager to know this increasingly in your own experience?"Because God is truly your Father, <u>you can expect</u> to rely on His Fatherhood constantly…"*

(Pg 13).

So you understand the emphasis on the need to expect guidance. Many of us fail to function at our God-ordained level because we fail to expect His guidance. It is as though in the Christian life you never receive what you do not expect. It is your expectation which moves you to ask.

Rev. Kenneth E. Hagin states "...*The Holy Spirit will use our spirit to guide and enlighten us as to God's will for our lives. He doesn't communicate with us directly through our minds or our body, because He dwells in our spirit. Therefore He communicates with us through our spirit...*" (Pg. 64) "*We can expect the Holy Spirit to guide and direct us so we can fulfill God's plan for our lives*" (Pg. 65).

From these we see how much we need to expect guidance in things large or small, significant or insignificant. As you expect guidance you will receive it. If you lack expectation to be guided, you will fail to receive guidance because God speaks to the person who will pay attention.

The Psalmist prayed, "*Guide me in Your truth and teach me, for You are God my Savior, and my hope is in you all day long*" (Ps 25:5). This prayer of his was based on his continuous hope (expectation) in the Lord throughout the day. Without his expectation in the Lord he could not receive any guidance. Expect God to guide you each moment. Anticipate, with delight, His guiding voice in your heart.

> "*Let the morning bring me word of your unfailing love, for I have put my trust in you. Show me the way I should go, for to you I lift up my soul.*"
> (Ps 143:8)

The Psalmist expected the dawn of each morning to bring him word of God's unfailing love. He expected to be shown (instructed about, directed, led on) the way his soul (will, mind, emotions) should go. In other words his expectations for the day were totally on the Lord. If you too would place your expectations on the Lord, He will definitely show you the way you should go. There is power in expectation to bring you guidance.

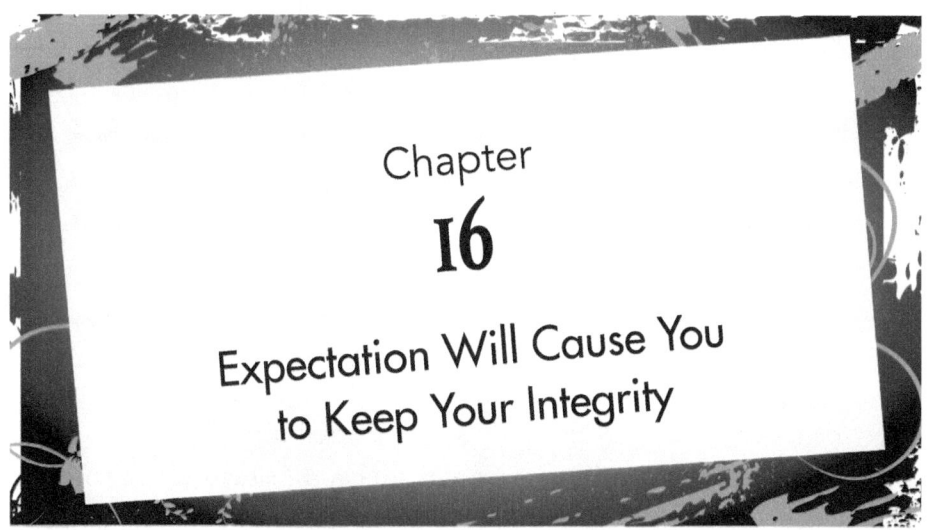

Chapter 16
Expectation Will Cause You to Keep Your Integrity

When a man has hope, he refuses to stain his hands or to soil his reputation no matter what happens to him. Integrity is a rare virtue which many have lost because of lack expectation. The capacity to maintain a blameless life, refusing to take advantage of anybody can only be upheld by your expectation. When it is lacking, there is the tendency to believe there is nothing at stake.

Your expectation for a heavenly home will cause you to uphold your integrity. Your expectation of restoration will cause you to keep yourself blameless, because you will not have anything deprive you of a heavenly reward when Christ comes. It will cause you to shun any behavior which will cause you not to be rewarded. Your expectation to reap a harvest from your acts of goodness will keep you from unwise actions and decisions.

When a man is looking forward to a greater blessing, when he has a picture of the great future God has in store for him, he refuses to play with or accept the offers of the world.

When Job was going through trials, what caused him to maintain his integrity was the expectation he had. In spite of all, even when he complained, deep inside he knew restoration was coming.

> "Then the LORD said to Satan, "Have you considered my servant Job? There is no one on earth like him; he is blameless and upright, a man who fears God and shuns evil. And he still maintains his integrity, though you incited me against him to ruin him without any reason."
>
> (Job 2:3)

Even though all he owned was gone, he held fast to his integrity because of hope for restoration. Even though his wife pressed him to throw away his integrity, seeing it as useless since according to her the situation was hopeless, Job still held on. Because the wife had no expectation for restoration, she had already given up and could say such evil.

> "God forbid that I should justify you: till I die I will not remove mine integrity from me.
> My righteousness I hold fast, and will not let it go: my heart shall not reproach me so long as I live."
>
> (Job 27:5-6 KJV)

Even though everybody else could not understand his ordeal Job decided that his integrity will remain a part of him. He decided that his conscience will never condemn him. That is, he lived a life and decided to continue to live a life of righteousness. If you too want to maintain a clear conscience as long as you live, put your expectation in Christ Jesus. This is what will keep you standing tall when you are all alone and everything is attempting to bowl you over.

The Psalmist prayed, *"May integrity and uprightness protect me, because my hope is in you"* (Ps 25:21). Do you want to be shielded, guarded, and protected by integrity and uprightness? Then put your hope in God.

The shrewd manager in the parable in Luke 16 resorted to firsthand dishonesty because he had no hope. He decided to cheat his master because, according to him, the future offered little after he lost his job. All his expectations in life were tied to his job. Hence taking away his job meant crumbling his whole world, so he decided to deal shrewdly with his master. If you place your hope in the wrong thing, you too will throw away your integrity when it is taken away.

How many young women have resorted to premarital sex because their hope in marriage crumbled? May it not be your portion. Maintain your integrity in all situations.

There is power in the right expectations to cause you to hold on to your integrity.

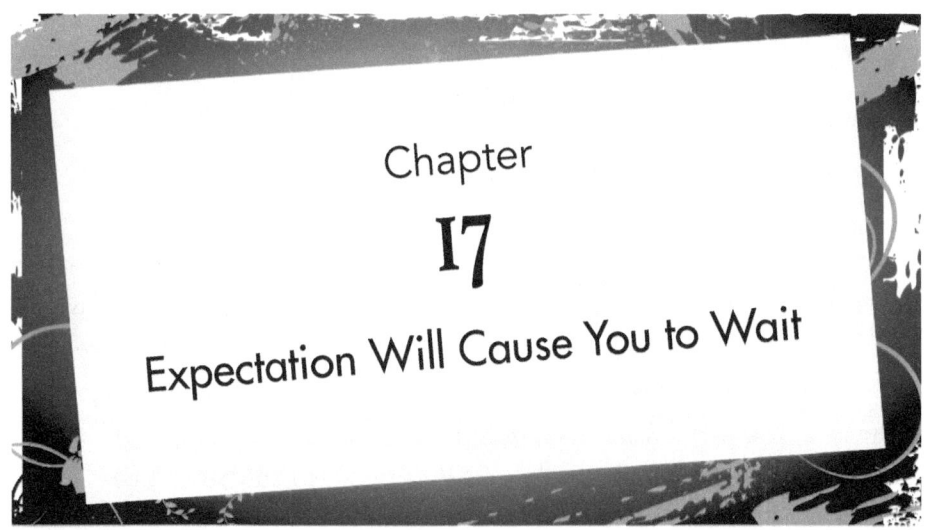

Chapter

17

Expectation Will Cause You to Wait

We live in the speed age and everyone has the tendency to want things to happen when, where, and how they have predetermined. However we come to realize that not everything is under one's control and certain situations demand that you wait if things must still be done according to the standards of God's word.

It is in such circumstances that many accuse God of being too slow to act. They tell God, at least by their attitude and actions, that they understand the situation better than Him. They ask Him to stay aside and watch them perform better than Him. This is what counts for many a wreckage of destinies littered all over the sea of life. Anyone who has truly put his or her hope in God will learn to wait for His proper time. When your hope is in God, you surrender everything to Him and move according to His timing. You understand that He has arranged your stops in life, likewise your starts and lifts. Lack of expectation accounts for the incapacity to wait!

> *"We wait in hope for the LORD; he is our help and our shield. In him our hearts rejoice, for we trust in his holy name. May your unfailing love rest upon us, O LORD, even as we put our hope in you."*
>
> (Ps 33:20-22)

Those whose expectations are in God understand He is their help and so they can do nothing without His help. Even when the help seems not to be coming they decide and prefer to wait. They understand that He is their protector and so in the face of danger they decide to wait on him.

Again, the Psalmist declared, *"I wait for the LORD, my soul waits, and in his word do I put my hope"* (Ps 130:5). In other words, when your expectations are based on the word of God, everything else can wait! You are prepared to wait for Him no matter how long it will take. You command your will power to wait! You command your emotions to wait! You command your mind to wait! For your whole soul must learn to wait. I like the way The Living Bible puts it. It says, *"That is why I wait expectantly, trusting God for help, for he promised. I long for Him more than sentinels long for the dawn."* (Ps 130:5-6, TLB)

Your expectations when based on the promises of God will cause you to wait, trusting His help that never fails. The Psalmist longed for (hoped, desired earnestly, expected) God's intervention more than the sentinels wait for the dawn. You know no matter what is happening, the sentinels cannot leave their watching posts until it is dawn. They may feel tired and may even want to go home but until it is dawn, they cannot and would not. What releases them is the dawn.

It is the same thing for those who have put their hope in God. No matter what happens they wait. In fact they cannot help but wait because they understand that when God steps in, what will be accomplished in the split of a second will never be accomplished in a lifetime acting ahead of Him. God's intervention is the dawn that releases them from their post of responsibility.

Paul wrote, *"[24]For in this hope we were saved. But hope that is seen is no hope at all. Who hopes for what he already has? [25] But if we hope for what we do not yet have, we wait for it patiently."* (Rom 8:24-25)

There is power in expectation to keep you waiting!

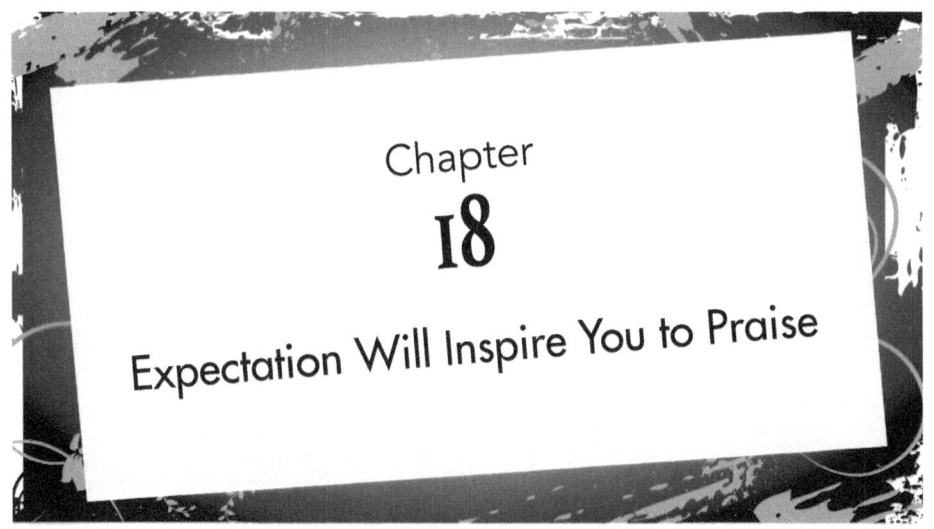

Chapter 18
Expectation Will Inspire You to Praise

Hope has the capacity to inspire you to praise the great and mighty God in any and every circumstance because no matter the situation you are going through, hope opens your eyes to the glories beyond each storm.

The Psalmist said, *"But as for me, I will always have hope; I will praise You more and more"* (Ps 71:14). In the face of trials, hope will cause you to praise, and increasingly praise God.

When Job was attacked and lost everything he owned to the storm, the Bible says, *"At this, Job got up and tore his robe and shaved his head. Then he fell to the ground in worship 21 and said: "Naked I came from my mother's womb, and naked I will depart. The LORD gave and the LORD has taken away; may the name of the LORD be praised.""* (Job 1:20-21). Why did Job put up such an attitude? What was the secret behind his strength and capacity to praise God? It is his expectation! He said: *"Though he slay me, yet will I hope in Him"*. (Job 13:15a). He hoped that what he was going through would turn out for his deliverance. That was the secret to his strength. So when you feel battered, praise the name of the Lord.

When you feel broken and
shattered, praise the Name of the Lord!

When you have lost everything to the
storms of life, praise the Name of the Lord!

When there is no one understanding you,
praise the Name of the Lord!

When you are rejected, despised and forsaken,
praise the Name of the Lord!

When you are scorned and ridiculed because of your faith and hope,
praise the Name of the Lord!

When all you seem to hear is bad news,
praise the Name of the Lord!

When you have been cheated and blackmailed,
praise the Name of the Lord!

When your husband doesn't love you any more,
praise the Name of the Lord!

When you are struggling to raise the kids all by yourself, praise the
Name of the Lord!

When your wife doesn't respect and obey you any longer, praise the
Name of the Lord!

When you have lost your job and you can't pay the bills, praise the
Name of the Lord!

When all seems fading, praise the Name of the Lord!

Expectation will Inspire You to Praise

When you think God is far away, praise the Name of the Lord!

Expectation will inspire you to praise Him in the good time, in the bad time, at all times.

Do you want your life to be filled with praise? Then place all your expectations in the Living God. When you expect the best even out of the worst, praise will become spontaneous because you will know that all things serve the Lord's purposes (Ps 119:91). Even the bad things that happen come to serve His purpose for your life. So you can praise Him when others don't see why you should be praising Him in such a circumstance. You praise Him because you know that, *"In him we were also chosen, having been predestined according to the plan of him who works out everything in conformity with the purpose of his will, [12] in order that we, who were the first to hope in Christ, might be for the praise of his glory."* (Eph 1:11-12).

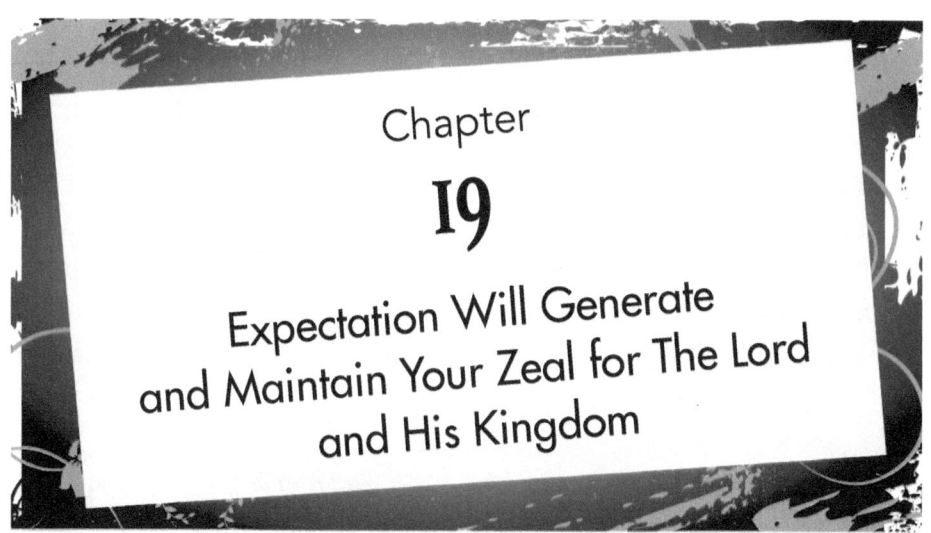

Chapter 19

Expectation Will Generate and Maintain Your Zeal for The Lord and His Kingdom

Zeal is one of the qualities lacking in the Christian circle today because expectation is equally lacking in many lives. People come to meetings (prayer, worship or teaching meetings) without any expectation and the result is a meeting with a predominantly lifeless atmosphere. Zeal or fervor or enthusiasm is what drives away lifelessness. However, zeal does not come like that. It is birthed and maintained by expectation in the heart.

Hope will make you to be earnest in your service. Paul said, *"⁶And now it is because of my hope in what God has promised our fathers that I am on trial today. ⁷This is the promise our twelve tribes are hoping to see fulfilled as they earnestly serve God day and night. O king, it is because of this hope that the Jews are accusing me."* (Acts 26:6-7). Let expectation birth in you earnestness in your service to God.

> *"Do not let your heart envy sinners, but always be zealous for the fear of the LORD. There is surely a future hope for you, and your hope will not be cut off."*
> (Pr 23:17-18)

When you have expectation for your future, when you have hope, you can turn your eyes away from the temporary prosperity of sinners. Many people lack in zeal because they serve the Lord with their eyes on the prosperity of the wicked. People lose the fear of God through envy of the gains of wickedness.

Do you want to be zealous for your God? Turn your eyes off worthless things that life seems to offer. Turn your heart from every manner of selfish gain to the hope that is in store for you when Christ will be revealed. Serve with zeal because you know that there is a reward awaiting you; a reward beyond the corruption of the fall. In encouraging the Apostles to maintain their zeal, the Lord Jesus Christ told them.

> *"^{1} Do not let your hearts be troubled. Trust in God; trust also in me. ^{2} In my Father's house are many rooms; if it were not so, I would have told you. I am going there to prepare a place for you. ^{3} And if I go and prepare a place for you, I will come back and take you to be with me that you also may be where I am."*
>
> (John 14:1-3)

This message was to encourage them not let go their zeal because of what was about to happen. He wanted them to lift their eyes beyond the troubled circumstances to the hope that was in store for them, even the hope of a new and enduring home. If you must serve the Lord, and serve Him with zeal, then your life must be full of expectation.

Paul, wrote, *"Never be lacking in zeal, but keep your spiritual fervor, serving the Lord."* (Rom 12:11).

> What is the secret to never be lacking in zeal?
> What is the secret to maintain your spiritual fervor?
> What is the secret to enthusiastic service to God?

As if in the same breath, he said, *"Be joyful in hope…"* (v 12). There is just one simple secret to all this, hope. When you have hope you will not only stay aglow but you will stay aflame, burning with ever increasingly brightness and zeal. And like the Messiah, you can say *"Zeal for your house consumes me"* (Ps 69:9).

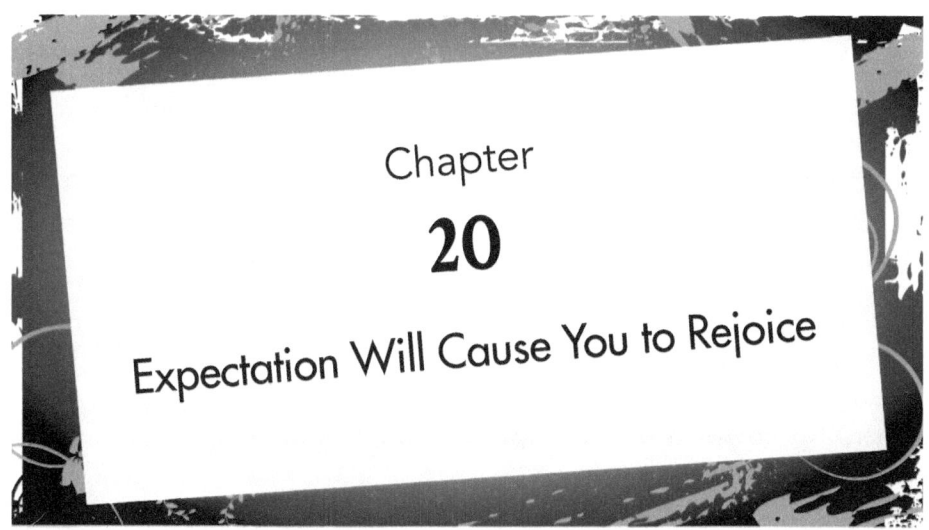

Chapter

20

Expectation Will Cause You to Rejoice

Expectation is the channel through which the oil of the joy in the Holy Ghost reaches our reservoir. Without expectation your reservoir will be empty and so your life will be void of the joy in the Holy Ghost.

Paul said,

> "^{1} Therefore, since we have been justified through faith, we have peace with God through our Lord Jesus Christ, ^{2} through whom we have gained access by faith into this grace in which we now stand. And we rejoice in the hope of the glory of God. ^{3} Not only so, but we^n also rejoice in our sufferings, because we know that suffering produces perseverance; ^{4} perseverance, character; and character, hope. ^{5} And hope does not disappoint us, because God has poured out his love into our hearts by the Holy Spirit, whom he has given us."
>
> (Rom 5:1-5)

What will keep you singing joyfully or rejoicing always is your hope. When you keep your focus on God's glory, such hope will cause you to rejoice even in the midst of suffering.

The Lord Jesus Christ said, *"^{11} Blessed are you when people insult you, persecute you and falsely say all kinds of evil against you because of me. ^{12} Rejoice and be glad, because great is your reward in heaven, for in the same way they persecuted the prophets who were before you."* (Matt 5:11-12).

He told His disciples to lift up their eyes beyond their troubles and persecutors to their reward in heaven. This is what generates joy in the midst of trials! When you are being insulted because of Christ, rejoice and be glad!

When you are being persecuted for righteousness sake, rejoice and be glad!

When they refuse to lease out that building to you because you are born again, rejoice and be glad!

When they refuse to employ you because you are born again, rejoice and be glad!

When they accuse you falsely because of your faith in Christ, rejoice and be glad!

When they say all kinds of evil against you, because you are a believer, rejoice and be glad!

Why should you rejoice in the midst of all these? Because, *"Great is your reward in heaven"*. When your eyes are lifted up to God, expectation will generate an awe-inspiring joy that will carry you through every sea of tests and trials.

This reminds me of the prophet Habakkuk. He was surrounded by injustice and wondered why everything seemed to disfavor the righteous. It was a time when wickedness thrived and judgment seemed to have fallen on the land.

So he said, *"Though the fig tree does not bud and there are no grapes on the vines, though the olive crop fails and the fields produce no food, though there are no sheep in the pen and no cattle in the stalls, yet I will rejoice in the LORD, I will be joyful in God my Savior."* (Hab 3:17-18)

There was agricultural crisis!

There was economic crisis!

There was social crisis!

Worst of all there was spiritual crises which let to all of the above!

But in the midst of all these, Habakkuk could rejoice in the Lord. It is obviously not because he did not care, but because he had learnt to lift up his eyes above everything and hope in the Lord.

Your business may be failing, you may not even know where the next meal will come from. You may not know how you are going to settle the bills and the rents. But because you have hope you rejoice in every circumstance. Expectation has power to generate joy, even joy unspeakable.

You shall not appear miserable anymore because expectation will generate joy that will change and transform your outlook from gloom to radiance. There is power in expectation!

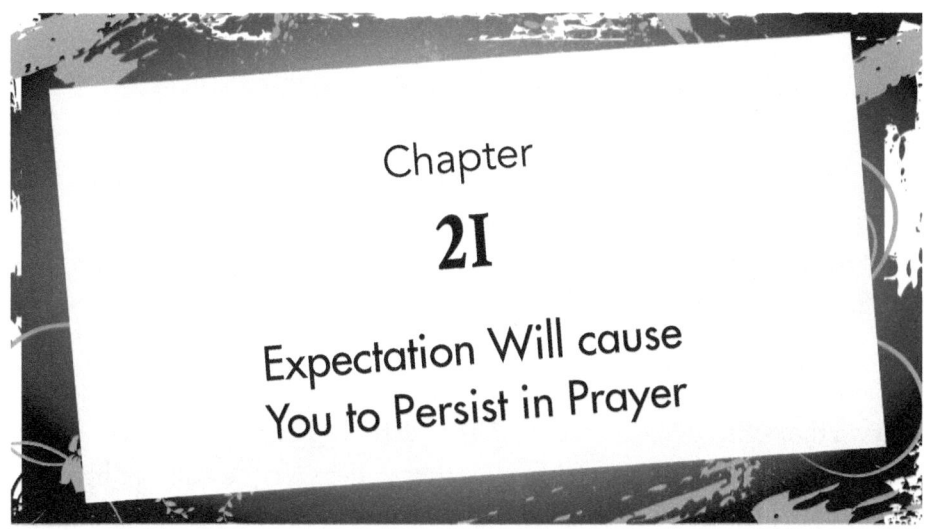

Chapter 21
Expectation Will cause You to Persist in Prayer

"But as for me, I watch in hope for the LORD, I wait for God my Savior; my God will hear me"

(Mic 7:7).

Another benefit that hope brings into a person's life is the ability to persist and prevail in prayer. Listen, many people talk about faith, but faith has nothing to act on when there is no hope. The very definition of faith as *"being sure of what we hope for and certain of what we do not see"* (Heb 11:1) shows that faith is only operational where there is hope. Though hope in itself is limited until faith is demonstrated on it, faith is inexistent without hope.

When you pray, you expect God to answer according to His faithfulness and promise in His word to answer prayer. Such expectation based on God's word does not fail. The prophet watched in expectation for the answer to his request. Because of his expectation he could wait for God's time, knowing that God was going to hear him.

On the contrary, some people pray without the slightest expectation of being heard and so they do not have the capacity to wait for the answer because it is expectation that births the capacity to wait without giving up. Expectation will cause you to pray and keep praying until the answer comes. Paul wrote: *"The widow who is really in need and left alone puts her hope in God and continues night and day to pray and to ask God for help."* (I Ti 5:5).

Why does she continue to pray night and day and ask God for help? Because of her hope in God! Her expectation for daily provision is no longer in a husband or any such thing but entirely in God. She knows that unless God acts nothing will happen and so she persists in asking for God's help.

Sometimes, prayer is like pregnancy and the result is like a baby. Naturally how do they call a pregnant woman? They describe her as an expectant mother! The expectation of becoming a mother and to carry a baby of her own causes her to endure the pains and discomfort of the gestation period. She does things with all care and caution because of her hopes for her baby. It is the same picture for one who has a prayer-burden. He persists until the baby (answer or result) comes forth because he is expectant of the results. He goes through the travail of persistence and prevalence because of his hope for the results.

Expectation will birth in you persistence and prevalence.

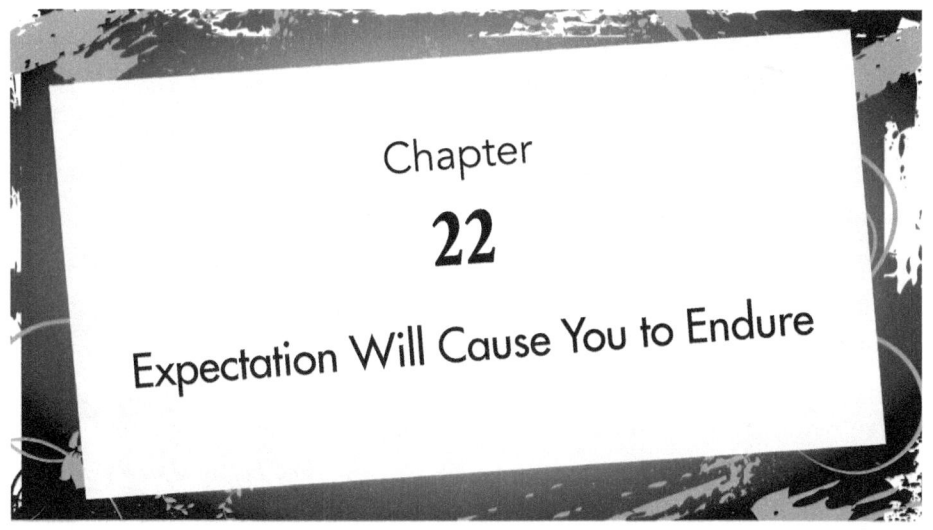

Chapter 22
Expectation Will Cause You to Endure

"We continually remember before our God and Father your work produced by faith, your labor prompted by love, and your endurance inspired by hope in our Lord Jesus Christ."

(I Th 1:3)

When your hope is in the Lord Jesus Christ, it will inspire you to endure the trails and pains that eventually come your way because of your faith. It is expectation that inspires endurance. Endurance doesn't just come like that, because one faces trials. About Moses, it is written: *"24 By faith Moses, when he had grown up, refused to be known as the son of Pharaoh's daughter. 25 He chose to be mistreated along with the people of God rather than to enjoy the pleasures of sin for a short time. 26 He regarded disgrace for the sake of Christ as of greater value than the treasures of Egypt, because he was looking ahead to his reward."* (Heb 11:24-26).

- He refused to be known as the son of Pharaoh's daughter
- He chose to be ill-treated along with the people of God
- He regarded disgrace for the sake of Christ as of greater value.

Why? *"...Because he was looking forward to his reward"*. Moses chose and endured all the above because of his expectation for a reward. Without this expectation, he couldn't have chosen to endure all that. Thus, we see that his expectation inspired in him endurance.

There are many things we as children of God have given up for the simple reason that we are expecting a reward. That is why Paul wrote, *"If only for this life we have hope in Christ, we are to be pitied more than all men"* (I Cor 15:19).

Look at what he went through because of his hope in resurrection

> *"29 Now if there is no resurrection, what will those do who are baptized for the dead? If the dead are not raised at all, why are people baptized for them? 30 And as for us, why do we endanger ourselves every hour? 31 I die every day--I mean that, brothers--just as surely as I glory over you in Christ Jesus our Lord. 32 If I fought wild beasts in Ephesus for merely human reasons, what have I gained? If the dead are not raised, "Let us eat and drink, for tomorrow we die."*
>
> (I Co 15:29-32)

> *"4 Rather, as servants of God we commend ourselves in every way: in great endurance; in troubles, hardships and distresses; 5 in beatings, imprisonments and riots; in hard work, sleepless nights and hunger; 6 in purity, understanding, patience and kindness; in the Holy Spirit and in sincere love; 7 in truthful speech and in the power of God; with weapons of righteousness in the right hand and in the left; 8 through glory and dishonor, bad report and good report; genuine, yet regarded as impostors; 9 known, yet regarded as unknown; dying, and yet we live on; beaten, and yet not killed; 10 sorrowful, yet always rejoicing; poor, yet making many rich; having nothing, and yet possessing everything"*
>
> (2 Co 6:4-10)

> *"23 Are they servants of Christ? (I am out of my mind to talk like this.) I am more. I have worked much harder, been in prison more frequently, been flogged more severely, and been exposed to death again and again. 24 Five times*

> *I received from the Jews the forty lashes minus one. ²⁵ Three times I was beaten with rods, once I was stoned, three times I was shipwrecked, I spent a night and a day in the open sea, ²⁶ I have been constantly on the move. I have been in danger from rivers, in danger from bandits, in danger from my own countrymen, ²⁷ in danger from Gentiles; in danger in the city, in danger in the country, in danger at sea; and in danger from false brothers. I have labored and toiled and have often gone without sleep; I have known hunger and thirst and have often gone without food; I have been cold and naked. ²⁸ Besides everything else, I face daily the pressure of my concern for all the churches."*
>
> (2 Co 11:23-28)

> *"Then Paul, knowing that some of them were Sadducees and the others Pharisees, called out in the Sanhedrin, "My brothers, I am a Pharisee, the son of a Pharisee. I stand on trial because of my hope in the resurrection of the dead."*
>
> (Acts 23:6),

> *"...and I have the same hope in God as these men, that there will be a resurrection of both the righteous and the wicked. ¹⁶ So I strive always to keep my conscience clear before God and man."*
>
> (Acts 24:15-16)

It is his hope in Christ Jesus that caused him to go through all that. He endured because he hoped to share in the glory of the kingdom.

About our glorious Lord, Jesus Christ, it is said that *"...for the joy set before him endured the cross scorning its shame, and sat down at the right hand of the throne of God"* (Heb 12:2b). It was not the cross in itself which gave Him joy and caused Him to endure, but what the cross was going to accomplish, even our salvation, deliverance, healing and restoration. He saw the end and so could joyfully endure the means, though painfully.

Expectation has power to generate endurance. Do you want to endure in all situations? Then it is time to put all of your expectations in the Lord Jesus Christ. Fix your eyes on Him and every other thing will fade away in the brightness of His countenance.

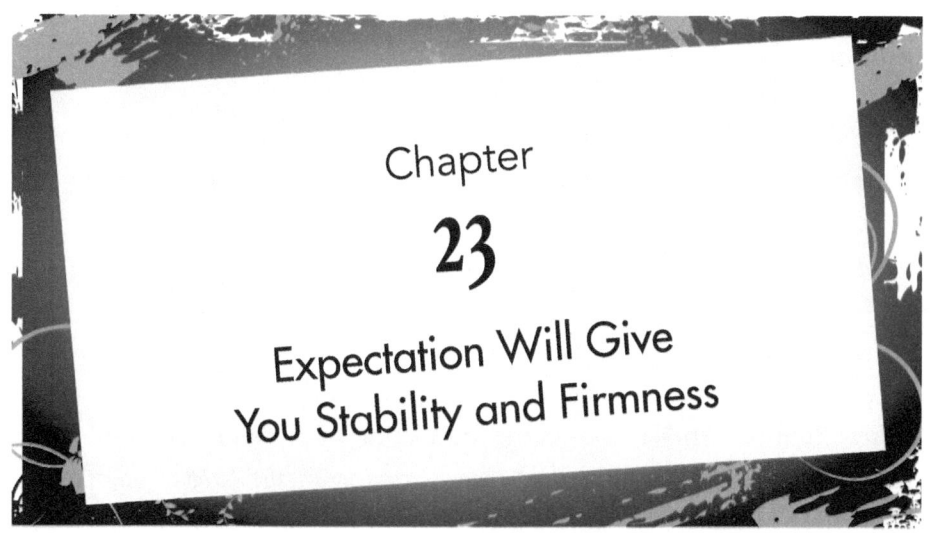

Chapter 23
Expectation Will Give You Stability and Firmness

*"My soul, wait thou only upon God; for my expectation is from him.
He only is my rock and my salvation: he is my defence; I shall not be moved.
In God is my salvation and my glory: the rock of my strength, and my refuge, is in God.
Trust in him at all times; ye people, pour out your heart before him: God is a refuge for us. Selah"*

(Ps 62:5-8 KJV)

"We have this hope as an anchor for the soul, firm and secure. It enters the inner sanctuary behind the curtain,"

(Heb 6:19)

People who truly have hope are not easily moved by circumstances. This is because hope acts as an anchor that prevents the soul from drifting in the stormy sea of life. In the most perturbing situation they find themselves with an inexplicable inner peace, calm and rest.

When God is the source of your expectations in life, you can wait and rest in total calmness amidst chaos, because you know that He is your Rock on which you can stand unmoved. He is the Rock to which your ship's anchor is tied and therefore you are not tossed about by circumstances, nor do you drift from your course.

Hope does not prevent storms from assailing you but makes you like the house that was built on solid ground such that *"The rain came down, the streams rose, and the winds blew and beat against that house; yet it did not fall, because it had its foundation on the rock"* (Matt 7:25).

We said before that faith only exists and can only be demonstrated because there is hope. Without hope, there is neither faith nor what faith should express itself on. And so hope is the foundation on which faith is built. Paul described ours as *"a faith and knowledge resting on the hope of eternal life, which God, who does not lie, promised before the beginning of time"*. (Tit 1:2).

Thus, hope is the bedrock of faith and knowledge you can hold on to. You can securely build on what you know when your expectations are based on what God has promised. Now the question might be asked, *"How does one have such a hope?"* Such hope has just one source and one way of being built in you.

God is the source of hope (Ps 62:5); it is He who imparts hope or causes expectations to be birthed in you. As you digest and assimilate scriptures, your faith increases. Why? Because the hope on which your faith rests has increased. Paul wrote to the Romans, *"For everything that was written in the past was written to teach us, so that through endurance and the encouragement from the scriptures we might have hope."* (Ro 15:4).

As you read and study the scriptures, you discover what God has promised you and begin holding on them. This will cause you to be firm in your pursuit of righteousness and love. (Ps 121)

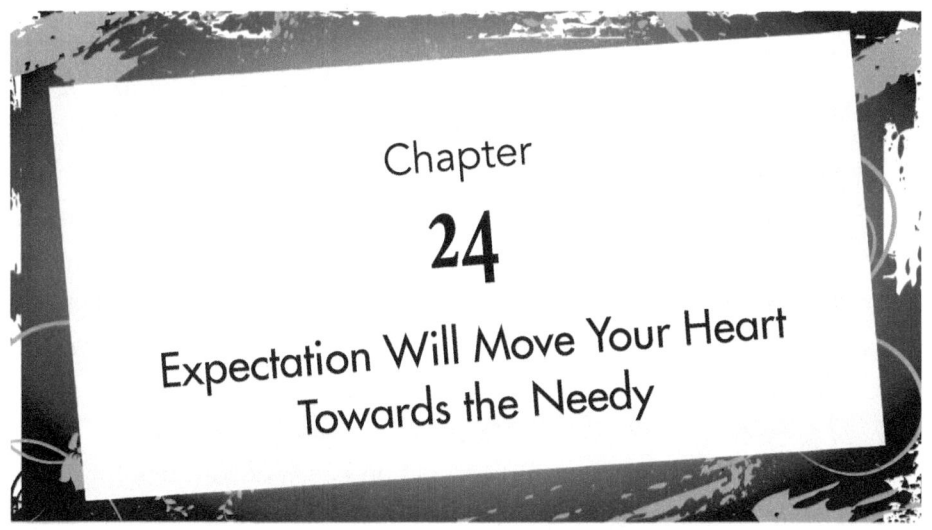

Chapter 24
Expectation Will Move Your Heart Towards the Needy

A man's heart will follow his expectations. That is why you must ensure that you have the right expectations. There are so many needy people around you. There are many who are suffering around you. Do you want to be compassionate towards these ones? Then expect God to do something for them through you! When you place yourself before the Lord as a channel of His blessing to mankind, you develop supernatural compassion for them. You begin to expect God to use you as an instrument to relieve their pain and suffering.

About the Lord Jesus, it is written: *"When Jesus looked up and saw a great crowd coming toward him, he said to Philip, "Where shall we buy bread for these people to eat?"* (Jn 6:5). If you too look up, you will notice a crowd of the hungry around you and become compassionate towards them. You will notice a crowd of the naked around you and seek to cloth them. You will notice a crowd of the hopeless around you and seek to provide hope. You will notice a crowd of the homeless around you and seek to provide them with shelter. You will notice a crowd of the oppressed around you and seek to relieve their oppression. Your eyes will behold the suffering, sick and possessed and you will offer yourself to God as a channel of His transforming power through the compassion which will be birthed in you.

What do you think motivated the early church, such that, *"All the believers were together and had everything in common. ⁴⁵ Selling their possessions and goods, they gave to anyone as he had need."* (Acts 2:44-45)? Nothing but compassion birth from expectation of the reward stored up for them in heaven. Compassion will cause you not to hoard anything. It will break the stronghold of greed and selfishness. It will push you to put the needs of others before yours. It is compassion that will cause you to *"share with God's people who are in need"* and *"practice hospitality"* (Ro 12:13).

Compassion will position you to trust God on behalf of someone for provision, healing, deliverance, or salvation. And it will make you a willing and available instrument in the hand of God for that particular need.

Talking about the gift of healing in relation to compassion, Smith Wigglesworth said,

> *"To have these gifts, I must bring myself into conformity with the mind and will of God. It would be impossible for you to have gifts of healings unless you possessed that blessed fruit of long-suffering. You will find that these gifts run parallel to what brings them into operation… Long-suffering is the grace Jesus lived in and moved in. He was filled with compassion, and God will never be able to move us to help the needy until we reach that place."*
>
> "Smith Wigglesworth on Healing" (Pg 142).

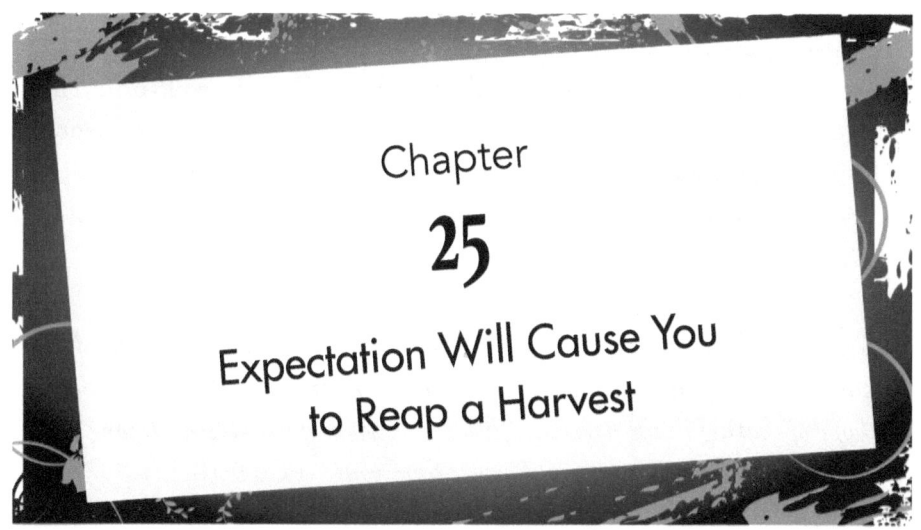

Chapter 25

Expectation Will Cause You to Reap a Harvest

Spiritual harvest is for those who expect to reap it. Your expectation of a harvest will get you to do all that is necessary, from the plowing, through sowing and every other thing that must be done for a harvest to be reaped. Spiritual harvest has never been, and will never be, something given to luck. It takes fervent, unwavering expectation to reap a harvest.

James wrote, *"Be patient, then, brothers, until the Lord's coming. See how the farmer waits for the land to yield its valuable crop and how patient he is for the autumn and spring rains."* (Jas 5:7)

Now how does the farmer wait for the land to yield its valuable crops? Does he just identify a piece of land and then expect it to yield a particular kind of crop for him to harvest? The answer is clearly a big *"No"*.

The farmer buys or rents a piece of land, identifies the correct season for planting and plows the field. After plowing the field he sows the right kind of seed. Now, because he does not have the rains under his controls, he is forced to patiently wait for the autumn and spring rains to water the seed sown and prepare the soil for a healthy growth. He keeps the field free of weeds and pests that may damage the crops and if need be applies the right kind of manure or fertilizer. All this is because he is expecting a harvest.

If you are expecting a harvest, a healthy spiritual harvest, your expectation will get you to take the right steps, do the right things and implement the right principles which will bring about that harvest. You cannot afford to sit and do nothing while expecting a miraculous harvest. You might as well wait till you pass to glory without reaping any such harvest.

Paul said, *"[10] Surely he says this for us, doesn't he? Yes, this was written for us, because when the plowman plows and the thresher threshes, they ought to do so in the hope of sharing in the harvest. [11] If we have sown spiritual seed among you, is it too much if we reap a material harvest from you?"* (I Co 9:10-11)

You see, when the plowman does his plowing, he is looking forward to one thing – sharing in the harvest. Because of his hope to share in the harvest, he does everything in his power to ensure that the field is properly plowed and in time so that the sower will sow in time.

The thresher too, when threshing, ensures that he does a proper job so that the grain does not remain in the stalks to be finally burned. He ensures that all of the grain is separated from the stalk. He ensures that he uses a good threshing sledge, sharpened to the correct degree.

Listen, your expectations will motivate you to work hard and keep your life in the good condition necessary for a good and healthy harvest. If you expect great things, you will attempt great things and therefore accomplish great things.

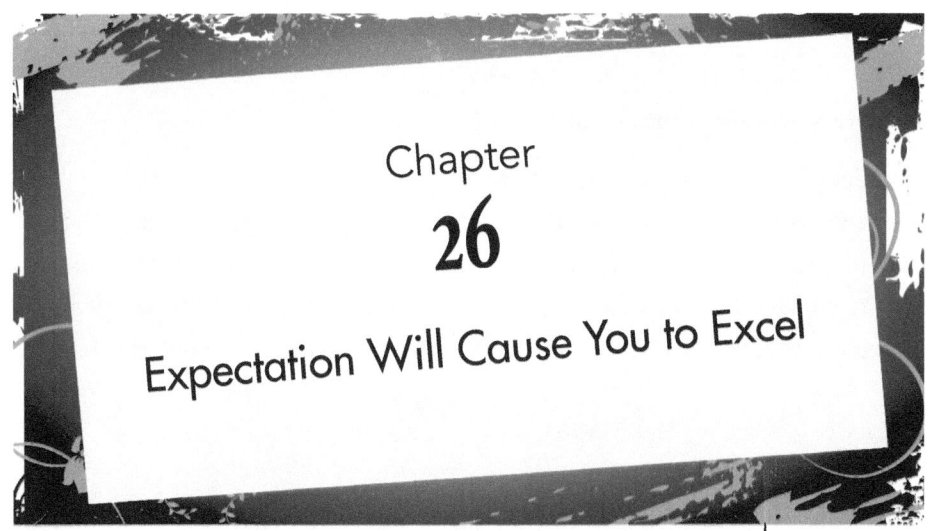

Chapter 26
Expectation Will Cause You to Excel

Lack of expectations accounts for many people's unconscious commitment to a life of mediocrity. Many people turn around the same spot year after year because of lack of expectation. They do not know the direction to move in because it is expectation that causes a man to receive direction in life. They fail to make any progress because the expectation which causes a person to break through barriers and obstacles in life is totally absent.

Lack of expectation deprives a man of vision and where there is no vision people are bound to perish in the prison of mediocrity and purposelessness.

Isaiah said, *"But those who hope in the LORD will renew their strength. They will soar on wings like eagles; they will run and not grow weary, they will walk and not be faint."* (Isa 40:31)

It will cause you to renew your strength.

In order for you to excel, you need a constant and continuous renewal of your strength, so as to keep up the pace. Your expectations which will cause you to be constantly refilled by tapping from the infinite reservoir that God has placed at your disposal. *"Those that hope in the Lord shall renew their strength."*

It will raise you above the ordinary.

Excellence is all about the capacity to perform far above the ordinary. If those who hope in the Lord will soar like eagles, then your expectations will cause you to excel. The eagle represents nothing but excellence. When you soar like an eagle you will rise to heights far above the ordinary. You will perform above the shades and clouds of life. That is what expectation will do for you.

You will not wear out

Many people give up because they grow weary in what they were doing, become faint and lose hope. Once hope is lost, all strength is sapped. Now, expectation is what will cause you not to wear out as you rise to new heights of excellence. It will shield you from the cold and pressures in the place of excellence. Those who hope in the Lord shall run and not be weary, walk and not faint. In fact expectation will cause you to finish strong.

Excellence is not just an occasional *"Head show"* in doing the extraordinary but the capacity to stay there and maintain the height that has already been attained. Many people quickly rise above mediocrity but fall even lower as fast as they rose. This is because, expectation was lost and so they could not be kept in that place of excellence. It is harder to keep yourself in the place of excellence than it is to get there. So know that once you get there, there is yet more work for you to do in order to stay there.

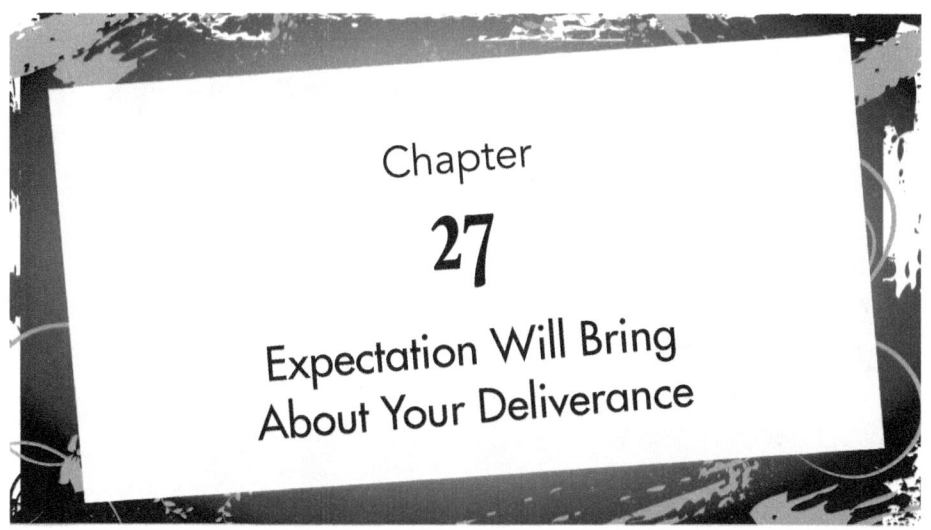

Chapter 27
Expectation Will Bring About Your Deliverance

Many things seek to take away one's God-bestowed capacities. Daily, the enemy spreads his nets, snares and traps, and due to negligence, you might get occasionally trapped. If he cannot keep us from working, he can get us caught in the web of false burdens and yokes that originate from him. Expectation will cause you to be constantly delivered from the pressures that weigh you down and from those hidden snares of the evil one.

Some get caught and remain there because they lack expectation. Expectation will cause you to yearn and cry out for deliverance if you find yourself in the wrong circumstance. Lack of expectation will bring about resignation and consequently enslavement.

There are financial, relational, mental and even spiritual entanglements which lurk daily at the corner, watching for who will get caught. The Apostle Paul wrote, *"He has delivered us from such a deadly peril, and He will continue to deliver us. On him we have set our hope that he will continue to deliver us"* (2 Co 1:10).

He wrote this chapter explaining the comfort he had received from the Lord in the midst of severe sufferings. He even mentioned the fact that he felt as though he had been sentenced to death because of the great pressure beyond his ability to endure. At a certain point, he even despaired of life. But once he regained his expectations and relied on God instead of himself his deliverance came. Paul now realized that in order to have his deliverance and remain delivered, he had to place his expectations for deliverance in the Lord.

I don't know the situation you find yourself entangled in, but if you refuse to give up or give in, if you maintain your expectation, if you lift up your eyes to the Throne of grace, then your deliverance will quickly appear.

Isaiah cried out,

> *"Strengthen the feeble hands, steady the knees that give way; say to those with fearful hearts, "Be strong, do not fear; your God will come, he will come with vengeance; with divine retribution he will come to save you."*
>
> (Isa 35:3-4)

If you know that your God will come for your deliverance and salvation, no matter what, then you will strengthen those hands that have grown weak. You will steady those knees that are giving way and every fear will be dispelled in the light of expectations.

When you have expectation for deliverance you can cry out like David, *"Arise, O LORD! Deliver me, O my God!"* (Ps 3:8a) because you know that: *"He will deliver the needy who cry out, the afflicted who have no one to help"* (Ps 72:12).

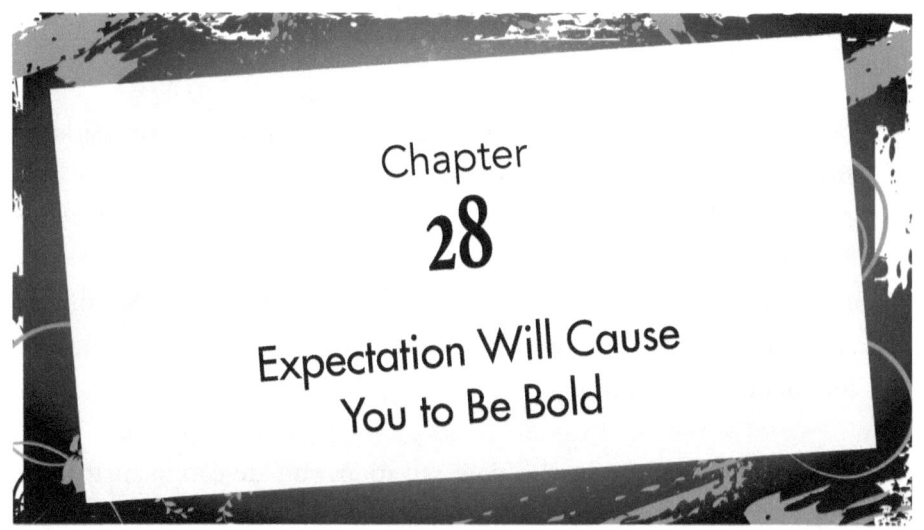

Chapter 28
Expectation Will Cause You to Be Bold

"Therefore, since we have such a hope, we are very bold."

(2 Co 3:12)

Expectations have the capacity to inspire boldness. Where there are expectations, the unknown can be faced with all boldness, risk can be taken with confidence, difficulties faced with bravery, and challenges confronted with great resolve. People who lack expectations are afraid to take determinant steps and make consequential moves. They are afraid to take risks that might bring about breakthroughs.

Obstacles diminish, barriers crumble, and difficulties give way in confrontation with a man full of the right expectations.

David said,

> *"The LORD is my light and my salvation-- whom shall I fear? The LORD is the stronghold of my life--of whom shall I be afraid? When evil men advance against me to devour my flesh, when my enemies and my foes attack me, they*

will stumble and fall. Though an army besiege me, my heart will not fear; though war break out against me, even then will I be confident"

(Ps 27:1-3).

When you know that the Lord is your light you are unafraid of any darkness that covers the path He is asking you to tread. You walk with confidence expecting that God will cause His light to shine on that path you are treading. You understand and know that *"The path of the righteous is like the first gleam of dawn, shining ever brighter till the full light of day."* (Pr 4:18). So, though darkness may cover the beginning of the path, because the Lord is your light you confidently expect His light to increasingly shine.

When you know that the Lord is your salvation, you are confident that He will save you from the fowler's snare and guide your feet in the path of triumph. With this you face the uncertain and the unknown with boldness. When you know the Lord is your stronghold, you are unafraid of the evil arrows that may be fired at you. You know that no harmful thing can pass into that stronghold. The Psalmist hoped for his enemies to always fail in their attacks no matter how many they were. You too should always expect the human and spirit agents of Satan to always stumble and fall in their attempts to get you.

God said to Jeremiah,

"Today I have made you a fortified city, an iron pillar and a bronze wall to stand against the whole land--against the kings of Judah, its officials, its priests and the people of the land."

(Jer 1:18)

You should live with the confidence of God's abiding presence, in you, with you, on you, and for you all the time, everywhere, in everything you do. You are unmoved by the threat of circumstance and people because your expectations in the Lord have generated boldness in you.

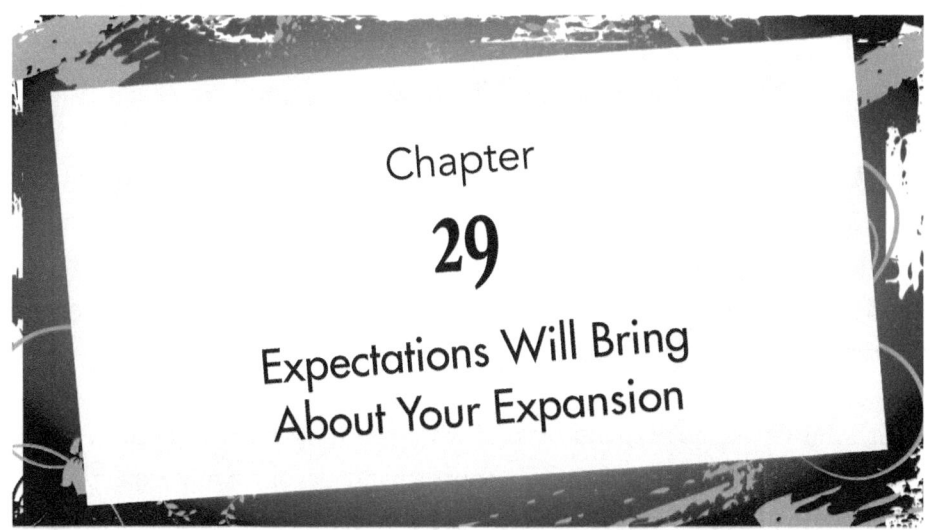

Chapter 29
Expectations Will Bring About Your Expansion

Some hundreds – nay, thousands of years ago, someone out of desperation, prayed asking God to expand his territory and sphere of influence. His request was granted because of his confident expectations.

> *"Jabez cried out to the God of Israel, "Oh! that you would bless me and enlarge my territory! Let your hand be with me, and keep me from harm so that I will be free from pain." And God granted his request."*
>
> (I Ch 4:10)

Jabez expected an enlargement of his territory - the domain of his influence financially, socially, materially, and spiritually. He wanted to be in total control of his environment and his request was granted.

He expected the hand of God to be with him, gracing all that he did and his request was granted. He expected a life free from pain and suffering he had so much experienced, and God met his expectations.

God was so pleased with Jabez's expectations for expansion that he caused him to become the owner of a city (See I Ch 3:55). Being the owner of the city meant an expansion in his financial domain. It meant an expansion socially, materially and otherwise. There is room for you too to expand and extend your sphere of influence whether spiritually, socially, financially, materially, intellectually or otherwise. All it takes is the right kind of expansions.

The Apostle wrote, *"Neither do we go beyond our limits by boasting of work done by others. Our hope is that, as your faith continues to grow, our area of activity among you will greatly expand, ^{16} so that we can preach the gospel in the regions beyond you. For we do not want to boast about work already done in another man's territory"* (2 Co 10:15-16)

Your ministry cannot expand beyond what you hope for it to become. Your business and other investments cannot expand beyond your expectations, at least not to any significant extent. There is tremendous power released to push back the walls of limitations and make room for expansion, when a man releases his expectations.

What expectations do you have for your ministry in the next five years? What expectation do you have for that business, five years from now? What expectations do you have for your family, five years from now? What expectations do you have for yourself as a social being for the next five years? What you become greatly depends on your expectations.

Do you want to have the right expectations? Then meditate on scripture. God has given all the promises in His word so that through them you and I can build confident expectations.

Now, when God tells you to; *"Enlarge the place of your tent, stretch your tent curtains wide, do not hold back; lengthen your cords, strengthen your stakes. For you will spread out to the right and to the left; your descendants will dispossess nations and settle in their desolate cities"* (Isa 54:2-3), He is asking you to get ready for a complete and total expansion in all areas of your life. Such expectations will push you to self-discipline and hard work, to actually make room for expansion. You see, when there is need for expansion all the unnecessary things are taken out of the way so that there can be room.

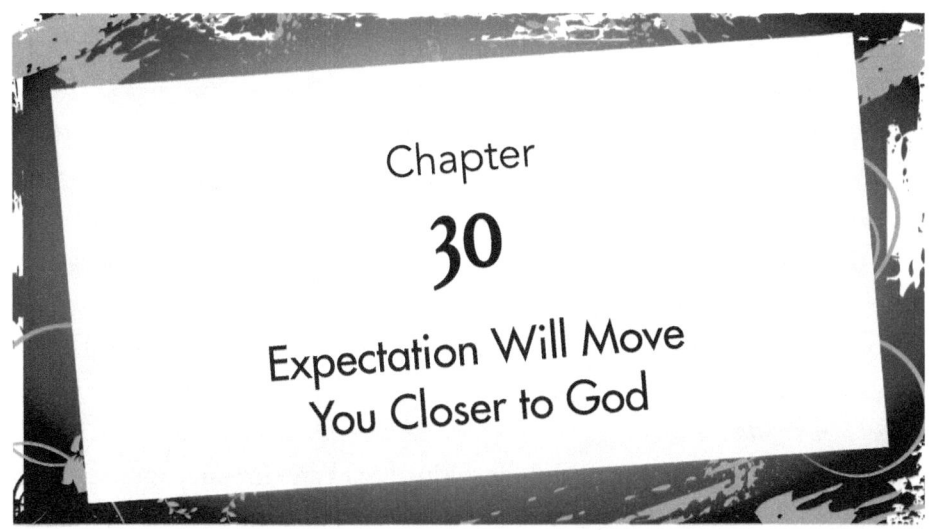

Chapter 30

Expectation Will Move You Closer to God

If your expectations of a given place or person are good and favorable, you will move closer to the place or individual. On the other hand, if your expectations of a place or person are bad or unfavorable, you will move away from the place or person.

A young man moves closer to a young woman because he sees in her the potentials of a good wife. He draws closer because he is expecting her to become his wife. On the other hand, he will separate himself from one who does not meet his qualities. A job seeker moves to a particular city because in that city he or she expects to find a job. He or she approaches a particular company because of his or her expectations of the company.

Your expectations of God will take you closer Him. Many people just wish they could draw nearer to God and find it difficult, not knowing the difficultly arose because of the lack of the right expectations of God. It is your expectations that will drive you nearer to God. Your expectations sustain you in your quest and pursuit of God.

The writer of Hebrews states: *"… and a better hope is introduced, by which we draw near to God"* (Heb 7:19). Your hope in God draws you nearer to God. The Lord Jesus Christ says: *"'Come to me, all you who are weary and burdened, and I will give you rest. ²⁹ Take my yoke upon you and learn from me, for I am gentle and humble in heart, and you will find rest for your souls. ³⁰ For my yoke is easy and my burden is light'"* (Mat 11:28-30). This means He expects us to come to Him with the expectation of being relieved of every weight. He is asking us to come to Him with expectations to find perfect rest and release from every kind of bondage.

If you expect God to relieve you of your weights and burdens, you will move closer Him in order to find that relief. He says: *"I am the bread of life. He who comes to me will never go hungry, and he who believes in me will never be thirsty."* (Jn 6:35) So He expects that our need for spiritual food and for our expectations to be satisfied eternally will cause us to move closer Him, to feed on Him until our souls are totally satisfied in Him. When He says: *"If anyone is thirsty, let him come to me and drink"* (Jn 7:37b), He expects that those who come to Him should come with expectation to be relieved of their thirst.

Your expectations to be satisfied and fulfilled in God will move you closer to Him.

Your expectations to be blessed and preserved by Him and in Him will move you closer God.

O, there are a thousand things you can expect in God which will cause you to move closer Him. Just respond to this invitation and you'll find yourself running to Him: *"Come, all you who are thirsty, come to the waters; and you who have no money, come, buy and eat! Come, buy wine and milk without money and without cost. Why spend money on what is not bread, and your labor on what does not satisfy? Listen, listen to me, and eat what is good and your soul will delight in the richest of fare."* (Isa 55:1-2).

What on earth do you think was the secret to David's desperate search for God, when he said, *"As the deer pants for streams of water, so my soul pants for you O God. My soul thirsts for God, for the living God. When can I go and meet with God"*? (Ps 42:1-2) It was all thanks to his expectations in God.

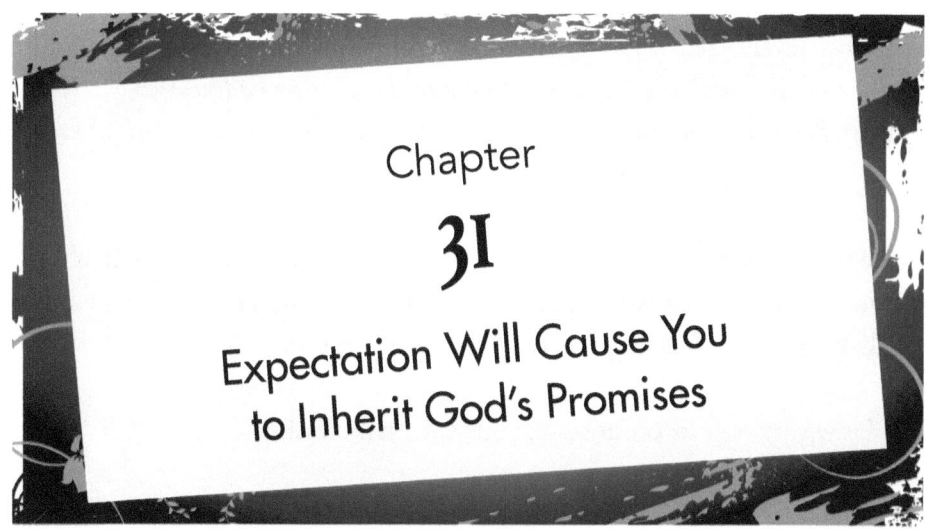

Chapter 31
Expectation Will Cause You to Inherit God's Promises

Many fail to inherit the promises given to us in the scriptures because of lack of expectations. What you expect is what you receive. Your expectations in life will determine your attitude towards things and people God brings your way, and above all, towards His word. And your attitude towards things or people determines what you receive from them.

Now, about Abraham, Paul wrote, *"[18] Against all hope, Abraham in hope believed and so became the father of many nations, just as it had been said to him, 'So shall your offspring be' [19] Without weakening in his faith, he faced the fact that his body was as good as dead--since he was about a hundred years old--and that Sarah's womb was also dead. [20] Yet he did not waver through unbelief regarding the promise of God, but was strengthened in his faith and gave glory to God, [21] being fully persuaded that God had power to do what he had promised."* (Rom 4:18-21) This tells you that all things did not work, apparently, in favor of God's promise to Abraham, but his expectations to see the promise fulfilled caused him to brave it through the adverse circumstances.

Your expectations of life give you tenacity in life. Why was his faith sustained? Because of his expectations to see God's promise fulfilled. Many people lose faith and fail to inherit God's promises because they also lose expectation. If you can keep to your expectations your faith can always be sustained even in the most severe trial. You see, Abraham's faith was strengthened because he was *"fully persuaded that God had power to do what he had promised"*. When you are persuaded about a thing, you can fully expect things to unfold favorably.

The Psalmist said, *"... those who hope in the LORD will inherit the land."* (Ps 37:9b). And how vast is the land you and I need to inherit. The vast land of God's promises of blessing for us; spirit, soul and body.

How vast are His promises for our spiritual blessing!

How vast are His promises for our financial blessing!

How vast are His promises for our family, work, business and friends.

How we need to hope in Him so as to have all these promises fulfilled in our lives. We said earlier that expectation will cause you to see the vastness of your inheritance. After you have seen the vastness of your inheritance, sustained expectation will cause you to inherit what you have beheld.

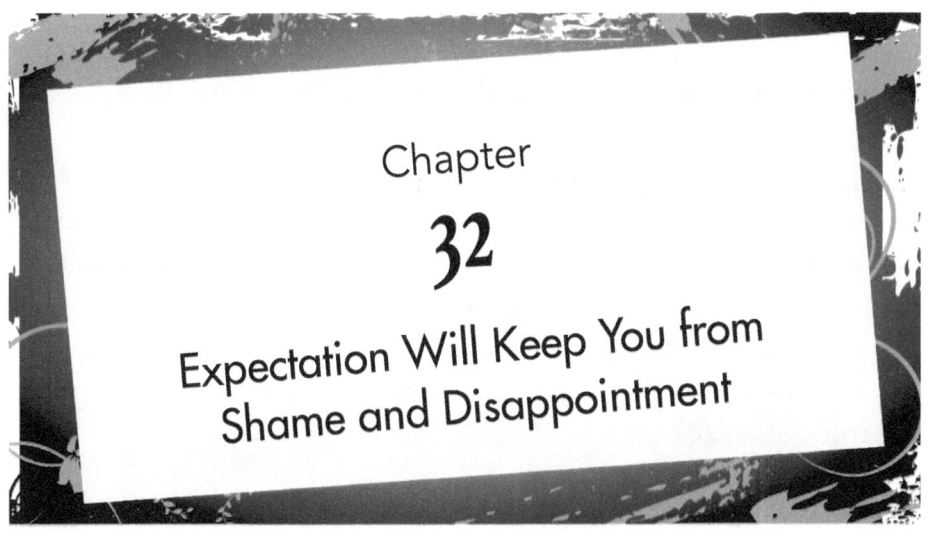

Chapter 32
Expectation Will Keep You from Shame and Disappointment

"Then you will know that I am the LORD; those who hope in me will not be disappointed."

(Isa 49:23c)

"No one whose hope is in you will ever be put to shame, but they will be put to shame who are treacherous without excuse."

(Ps 25:3)

"And hope does not disappoint us, because God has poured out his love into our hearts by the Holy Spirit, whom he has given us."

(Ro 5:5)

The Bible says, *"Hope deferred makes the heart sick, but a longing fulfilled is a tree of life"* (Pr 13:12). Hope in the wrong people and the wrong things will always prove unreliable. There are many broken hearts, shattered and battered lives because of wrong expectations. When the heart gets sick, many things fall apart in the life because the coordination center for spiritual affairs gets destabilized.

We said before, that when we build our expectations on the word of God, nothing in this world can shake them because they are built on the solid foundation of the unchanging word of God. Expectations placed in things or people will change as the people or things change and will finally crumble.

God says those who hope in Him will not be disappointed. If all your expectations are in the Lord, disappointment will never, under any circumstance, be part of your daily life. God will always prove to those who trust absolutely in Him that He is worthy to be trusted. He is too faithful to fail and too reliable to disappoint. There is a place where you can live a disappointment-free life, a place where all your longings are fulfilled. And that is the place where you live in absolute trust in God Almighty.

The Psalmist puts it more emphatically in the verse just cited above. When he says *"no one"*, he means just that. It does not depend on your color, race, qualification, age, spirituality, anointing or whatsoever. As long as your hope (expectation) is in the Lord, your life will be void of shame. God is the only sure basket into which you can place all your eggs and drive on the roughest road without fear of them breaking.

There are many things you have denied yourself and yet you can walk with your head high, without any shame because of your expectations to be rewarded by the Lord Jesus Christ for all that you have given up for His Name's sake.

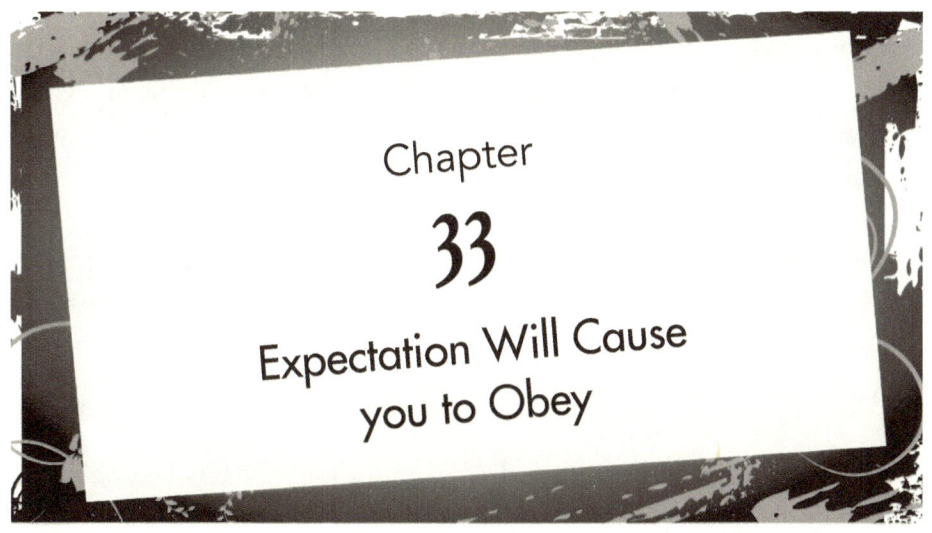

Chapter 33
Expectation Will Cause you to Obey

When you are full of expectations, you will live an obedient life. Expectations have power to inspire obedience and generate in a man or woman, boy or girl the capacity to obey.

> *"By faith Abraham, when called to go to a place he would later receive as his inheritance, obeyed and went, even though he did not know where he was going. By faith he made his home in the Promised Land like a stranger in a foreign country; he lived in tents, as did Isaac and Jacob, who were heirs with him of the same promise. For he was looking forward to the city with foundations, whose architect and builder is God."*
>
> (Heb 11:8-10)

Verse 10 gives us the reason for his faith and consequent obedience. You know the Bible says we have been called to an obedience which stems from faith (Rom 1:5). And hope is what faith is built on. So Abraham obeyed because *"he was looking forward..."* In other words he was full of expectations. His expectations caused him to see beyond the pang of separation to the glories that were his after he obeyed.

You too can live obediently if you allow the Holy Spirit to birth in you expectations. Expectations have power to cause you to obey. When you read the word of God, what causes you to put it into practice is your expectations tied to what you are reading. Behind every instruction is a blessing or reward. And usually the more painful the obedience required, the greater the reward and blessing hidden behind that instruction.

Those who learn to look beyond the instruction to the blessing of obedience will be joyful. Nothing brings joy like after you have obeyed, even when you did not understand why you should obey. Then you rejoice and thank the Lord that He granted you the grace to obey Him.

Most often, after you have obeyed, even though all else was beckoning on you to disobey, you just can't help but shed tears of joy for the grace God granted you to obey. There is power in obedience, and it is the power of expectations that causes a man to obey even when your human understanding and natural evidences call for you to do the contrary.

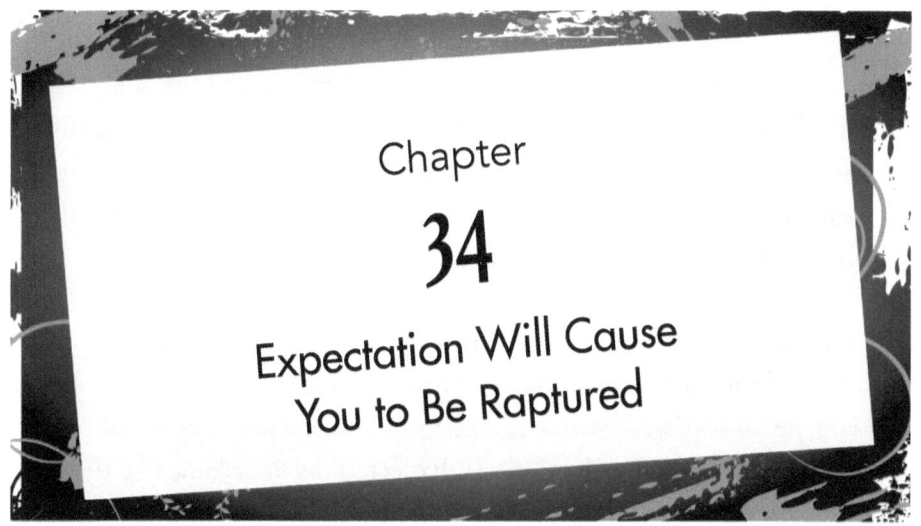

Chapter 34
Expectation Will Cause You to Be Raptured

The truth is that the Lord Jesus is coming for those who are waiting for Him!

He is coming to reward those who are waiting for Him!

He is coming to bring salvation to those who are waiting for Him!

He is coming to bring deliverance to those who are waiting for Him!

He is coming to take home, those who are waiting for Him!

The Bible says, *"Now there is in store for me the crown of righteousness, which the Lord, the righteous Judge, will award to me on that day--and not only to me, but also to all who have longed for his appearing."* (2 Ti 4:8), and again, *"so Christ was sacrificed once to take away the sins of many people; and he will appear a second time, not to bear sin, but to bring salvation to those who are waiting for him."* (Heb 9:28). The Lord Jesus' second coming is only for those who are waiting for (longing for, expecting) Him. Are you expecting the return of the Lord Jesus? Your expectation in Him will connect you to the rewards He is coming with.

Also because you are waiting for (expecting) Him you will live a *rapturable* life. In other words, you will live your life, consistently being in a qualified condition to go with Him should He appear at any time. He Himself asked us to be watchful for His return. And when you are watchful you guard against all that can disqualify you for rapture.

The Bible says, *"Dear friends, now we are children of God, and what we will be has not yet been made known. But we know that when he appears, we shall be like him, for we shall see him as he is. ³ Everyone who has this hope in him purifies himself, just as he is pure."* (1 Jn 3:2-3). Expectations to become like the Lord Jesus at His appearing will cause you to be pure. Lack of these expectations can cause you to be relegated to the class of those living in perpetual compromise.

Elsewhere in the Book, it is written: *"But in keeping with his promise we are looking forward to a new heaven and a new earth, the home of righteousness. So then, dear friends, since you are looking forward to this, make every effort to be found spotless, blameless and at peace with him."* (2 Pe 3: 13-14)

So it is your duty to make the effort. Not just an effort but every (possible, or known) effort to be spotless and blameless and at peace with the Lord. Your expectations to be ruptured will cause you to ensure that there is no barrier between the Lord and you or some other believer and you.

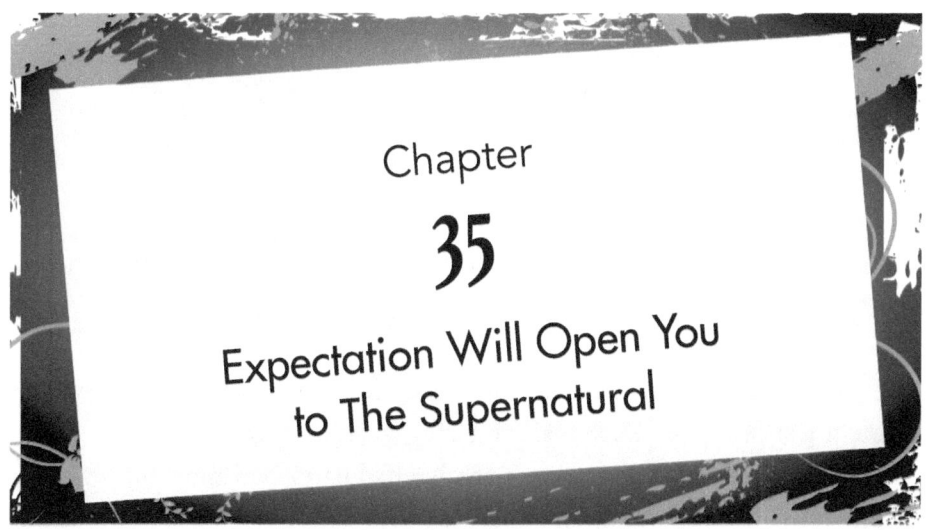

Chapter 35
Expectation Will Open You to The Supernatural

Life is greatly limited, progress slow and sometimes greatly impeded when one's view is limited to the natural. Often, a glimpse of the divine supernatural brings tremendous, unprecedented change into one's life and environment. Seeing into the supernatural is seeing through the eyes of God.

When you see through the eyes of God, your outlook and reaction to situations change for the better. Remember when the Arameans came to take the prophet Elisha captive because the Aramean king had been told all his plans to defeat Israel by capturing their king were being foiled by Elisha.

When Elisha's servant got up early in the morning he was panic-stricken to find their whole compound surrounded by Aramean troops. His master, the prophet was most unmoved because he saw into the divine supernatural. He saw the situation through the eyes of God and so was confident. In other to birth the same confidence in his servant, he prayed for the Lord to open the servant's eyes so he too could see into the supernatural.

> "Don't be afraid," the prophet answered. "Those who are with us are more than those who are with them." And Elisha prayed, "O LORD, open his eyes so he may see." Then the LORD opened the servant's eyes, and he looked and saw the hills full of horses and chariots of fire all around Elisha."
>
> (2 Ki 6:16-17)

When his eyes were opened he had to look before he could see the horses and chariots of fire. Expectation will open your eyes to the divine supernatural and change your outlook.

After the captivity, when the exiles returned, the Lord had to encourage them through the prophets, Zachariah and Haggai. One way He did this was to give the prophets an understanding of what had happened and what was happening in the supernatural. The following verses point to the fact that it was the prophet's expectations that opened him up to the supernatural!

> "[18] Then I looked up--and there before me were four horns! [19] I asked the angel who was speaking to me, "What are these?"
> He answered me, "These are the horns that scattered Judah, Israel and Jerusalem."
> [20] Then the LORD showed me four craftsmen. [21] I asked, "What are these coming to do?"
> He answered, "These are the horns that scattered Judah so that no one could raise his head, but the craftsmen have come to terrify them and throw down these horns of the nations who lifted up their horns against the land of Judah to scatter its people."
>
> (Zech 1:18-21)

> "[1] Then I looked up--and there before me was a man with a measuring line in his hand! [2] I asked, "Where are you going?"
> He answered me, "To measure Jerusalem, to find out how wide and how long it is."
>
> (Zech 2:1-2)

Verse 18 says, *"Then I looked up…"*, likewise verse 1 of chapter 2. In other words *"then I was filled with expectation…"* Your expectations will open you up to the Divine supernatural which will give you a supernatural understanding of things that are happening and that will happen in your life and environment.

You can go to bed expecting to be spoken to by the Lord through dreams and visions. Dreams open you up to what is happening in your life and environment. In fact I do take my dreams very seriously because through them, God has often showed me the real people with whom I am dealing. Expect to be shown things by God. From this day may you live in utmost expectation to receive supernatural guidance.

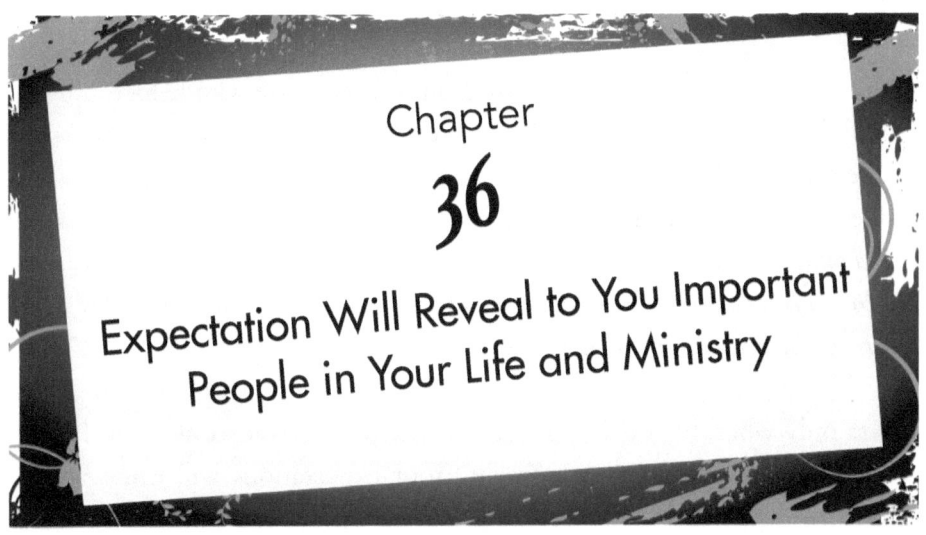

Chapter 36

Expectation Will Reveal to You Important People in Your Life and Ministry

The kind of people you relate with greatly influences what you become in life. Some people or relationships are important and indispensable for the fulfillment of your destiny. Expectation reveals and even links you to people who matter in your life. In your daily life, expect God to bring the right people across your path. Your attitude to the strangers you meet determines a lot.

When you live with the expectation of meeting the right persons for the fulfillment of your destiny, you will treat every encounter with godly care. Many people miss life-changing encounters and forfeit their blind date with destiny because they do not have expectations in that direction.

About Isaac and Rebecca, the Bible says, *"⁶³ He went out to the field one evening to meditate," and as he looked up, he saw camels approaching. ⁶⁴ Rebekah also looked up and saw Isaac."* (Gen 24:63-64). It was by looking up, that is, by being full of expectation that they noticed each other, hence were bonded together in a relationship that changed the course of history. Your expectations will bring change in your life and destiny. They may link you to your life partner, ministry partner, mentor, or some other relationship of influence and consequence.

Jehu's expectations did reveal to him his loyalists; those who helped him accomplish God's assignment. With the commission to wipe out the house of the idol worshipper Ahab, Jehu went to Jezreel where Jezebel the witch resided. When he got there, the Bible says, *"³² He looked up at the window and called out, "Who is on my side? Who?" Two or three eunuchs looked down at him. ³³ "Throw her down!" Jehu said. So they threw her down, and some of her blood spattered the wall and the horses as they trampled her underfoot."* (2 Ki 9:32-33).

It was only when he looked up that he saw people who could help him in accomplishing his divine assignment. Your expectations will cause you to know your loyalists. It will reveal to you those who will remain true to you as you seek to fulfill your divine assignment. Live daily, in expectation of such encounters and at the right time the Lord will bring them your way. When you live with such expectations you will learn to maximize opportunities, and treat with utmost respect, the openings the Lord gives you to meet people of consequence, even for brief moments.

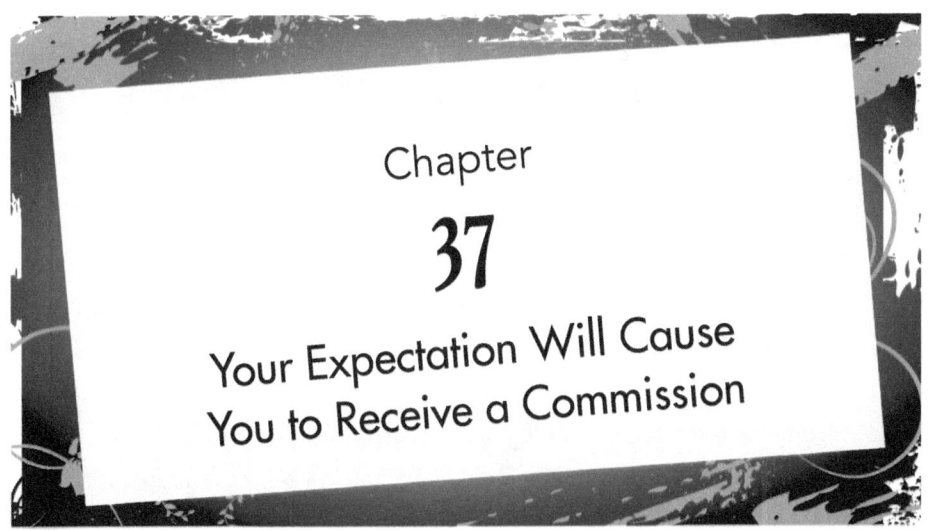

Chapter 37
Your Expectation Will Cause You to Receive a Commission

It is a shameful thing to find many idle in the household of God because they do not know what God has called them to do. The truth is that you can only find fulfillment in discharging your God-ordained responsibility in His house. Many get frustrated because they try to function in an office when they have not received the necessary unction to function there.

The reason many have nothing doing is that they have not asked the right questions. They have not asked the right questions because they have not sought to know. And they have not sought to know because of lack of expectations.

It is expectation that makes you curious to know. It is your curiosity that pushes you to ask the right questions and asking the right questions reveals what God wants you to do. In my book *"Fulfilling Your Destiny"*, I wrote extensively on how to receive a commission. It all begins with expectations or desire. Desire gives birth to curiosity and curiosity leads to great and life-changing discoveries.

In his life changing encounter with the Master on the Damascus road, Paul because of his expectation asked the right question, and he, was told what he had to do and later on, he received his commission. What would have happened had Paul failed to ask the right question?

This is his account of that encounter:

> *"⁶About noon as I came near Damascus, suddenly a bright light from heaven flashed around me. ⁷I fell to the ground and heard a voice say to me, 'Saul! Saul! Why do you persecute me?'*
> *⁸'Who are you, Lord?' I asked.*
> *"'I am Jesus of Nazareth, whom you are persecuting,' he replied. ⁹My companions saw the light, but they did not understand the voice of him who was speaking to me.*
> *¹⁰ "'What shall I do, Lord?' I asked.*
> *"'Get up,' the Lord said, 'and go into Damascus. There you will be told all that you have been assigned to do.'"*

(Acts 22:6-10)

The first question he asked, *"Who are You Lord?"*, showed that he expected a personal knowledge of the Master. Is there any doubt Paul knew Him so closely?

The second question, *"What shall I do, Lord?"*, expressed his expectation to be used by God. He knew there was something God wanted him to do. The Lord decided to increase that expectation in Paul and so told Paul: *"get up and go into the city and you will be told what you must do"* (Acts 9:6). On his way to the city, Paul expected to receive his commission. Because of his expectations, Ananias could tell him *"¹⁴The God of our fathers has chosen you to know his will and to see the Righteous One and to hear words from his mouth. ¹⁵ You will be his witness to all men of what you have seen and heard. ¹⁶ And now what are you waiting for? Get up, be baptized and wash your sins away, calling on his name."* (Acts 22:14-16).

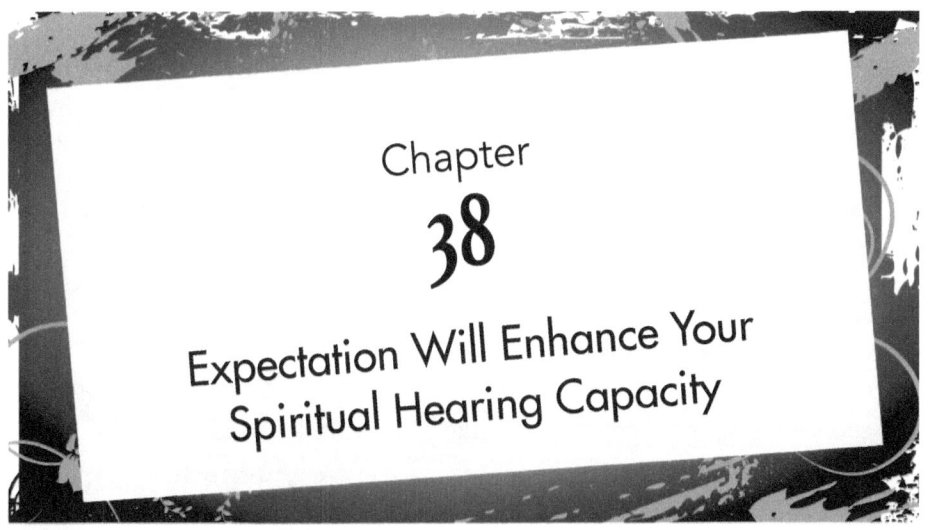

Chapter 38
Expectation Will Enhance Your Spiritual Hearing Capacity

When a man expects to hear, he listens with attention. Your expectation to hear God speak to you will cause you to develop a keen listening hear and put yourself constantly in a position to hear Him clearly. Many people fail to hear or distinguish the voice of the Spirit because they do not expect to hear Him speak.

I must confess that when I live in expectation to hear the Holy Spirit speak to me I have often heard His voice even in the midst of external noise. On the contrary when I do not expect Him to speak I only realize later that He had spoken but I couldn't decipher because I didn't expect Him to speak. This places a great responsibility on you to live continuously expecting to hear the Lord.

In the book of Revelations John said, *"Then I looked and heard…"* (Rev 5:1). It is in looking (expecting) that he heard. If he did not look (expect) he would not hear. Your expectation will cause you to hear the right things.

> *"The Sovereign LORD has given me an instructed tongue, to know the word that sustains the weary. He wakens me morning by morning, wakens my ear*

> *to listen like one being taught. The Sovereign LORD has opened my ears, and I have not been rebellious; I have not drawn back."*
>
> (Isa 50:4-5)

Get up each morning with an expectation to receive instructions from the Lord. Expect Him to waken and open your ears so that you can hear Him clearly. It is expectation that will cause you to pray *"O Lord, sharpen my spiritual hearing, enhance my capacity to hear even the faintest whisper from You."*

You see that lack of expectations causes many of us to miss vital instructions. It may take just a simple whisper to save your life from the pit, trap or snare the enemy has kept for you. It may take just a whisper to change your future for the better. Without a keen listening ear you are greatly deficient.

The Lord invites you to *"call to me and I will answer you and tell you great and unsearchable things you do not know"* (Jer 33:3). So when you call to Him expect Him to speak, and then listen to what He says to you. Unless you listen you will not benefit from it.

Do you remember the boy Samuel? Since he was not expecting God to speak to him, when He called Samuel ran to Eli. God only spoke clearly to him when he expected to hear God by answering *"speak Lord for your servant is listening"* (1Sa 3:10c). In the position of close attention, expecting God to speak, , the next verse says, *"And the LORD said to Samuel…"*. Your expectation will enhance your hearing capacity.

Chapter 39
Further Truths About Expectations

Expectation Is Your Calling

"I pray also that the eyes of your heart may be enlightened in order that you may know the hope to which he has called you, the riches of his glorious inheritance in the saints"

(Eph 1:18)

God has called you to a hope (an expectation) in Him. When you fill your life with expectation based on God's word you are fulfilling your calling.

Expectation Guarantees You A Future

"For I know the thoughts that I think toward you, saith the LORD, thoughts of peace, and not of evil, to give you an expected end "

(Jer 29:11 KJV).

God has an expected end for you. As you live in expectation to move into what God has ordained for you the first thing you need to do is expect it.

Expectation Comes From God

"Find rest, O my soul, in God alone; my hope comes from him." (Ps 62:5)

You cannot generate expectation on your own. God is the source of all right expectations. When you spend time with Him He gives you great expectations.

Expectation Must Be In The Name Of Jesus

"In his name the nations will put their hope." (Mt 12:21)

His Name is the only sure foundation for anything. If you must have expectations that bring lasting results, then all must be in His Name.

Expectation Is A Sign Of Dependence.

> *"I lift up my eyes to you, to you whose throne is in heaven. As the eyes of slaves look to the hand of their master, as the eyes of a maid look to the hand of her mistress, so our eyes look to the LORD our God, till he shows us his mercy."*
> (Ps 123:1-2)

When you place your expectation in God, when you look up to Him for protection, provision, direction etc., you are demonstrating your dependence on the Lord. And the Lord is pleased when you show this kind of dependence on Him.

Expectation Must Be Constant and Persistent

> *"'Go and look toward the sea,' he told his servant. And he went up and looked.
> "'There is nothing there,' he said. Seven times Elijah said, 'Go back'. The seventh time the servant reported, 'A cloud as small as a man's hand is rising from the sea.'*

Further Truths About Expectations

> *"So Elijah said, 'Go and tell Ahab, "Hitch up your chariot and go down before the rain stops you."' Meanwhile, the sky grew black with clouds, the wind rose, a heavy rain came on and Ahab rode off to Jezreel."*
>
> (I Ki 18:43-45)

For you to get lasting results you have to constantly and continuously expect. The servant was consistent and persistent in his lookout until the desired cloud was seen.

Expectation Provides A Ground For Faith To Act.

> *"So they took away the stone. Then Jesus looked up and said, "Father, I thank you that you have heard me."*
>
> (Jn 11:41)

It is in looking up that Christ Jesus demonstrated His expectations for the Father to grant His request. Expectations expressed, provide a ground for faith to act.

Chapter 40
Beware of Wrong Expectations

Expectations have power; not only do right expectations have power but also, wrong expectations do have negative power. *"When is an expectation wrong?"* is the question you may be asking at this time. We said before that our expectations must be based on the word of God. Right and concrete expectations are based on what God has said or is saying about a situation. To expect things God has not promised is to build castles in the sky.

Nothing can become as frustrating and disappointing as having the wrong kind of expectations. The Bible says in Proverbs 13:12 that *"Hope deferred makes the heart sick, but a longing fulfilled is a tree of life"*. In other words expectations not met will make the heart (spirit) sick. And there are many people today who are sick on the inside because of the wrong expectations which never get fulfilled.

Let us see cases in which people had the wrong expectations and what happened:

Expectations beyond what has been agreed

Read Mt 20:1-10

Here is the story of a man who decided to recruit workers for his vineyard. The first set recruited had an agreement with him for a certain sum of money in return for their service the whole day. This guy hired workers at different times of the day to work in the same vineyard with the others. The only difference is that with the ones hired later, he was to pay them whatever he wanted. Now when the time for payment came at the end of the day he decided to begin payment with those who were hired last and gave them each the same sum he agreed with the ones hired first.

The Bible says, *"So when those came who were hired first, they expected to receive more. But each one of them also received a denarius."* (Mt 20:10). The truth is these men had an expectation to receive something more but the expectation was wrong because it had no foundation. And as such they were disappointed and began to grumble. You see what wrong expectations can do! There are too many people angry at the Lord; they spend their time murmuring and grumbling. They fuss and cuss, rant and rave at God because God has not met their expectations. God is not bound to meet expectations that did not originate from Him or His word. God's word to us is His agreement with us sealed with the blood of His Son, the eternal King, Jesus Christ.

Anything which is not founded and grounded on what the word says is a wrong expectation. Do not base your expectations on what you see God doing in the lives of others. When some people see God using someone in a particular way, they begin praying and fasting that God should use them that same way. And such people pray and fast throughout their lives without receiving what they expect because God never promised to use all of us in the same way. He says in His word that we all have different gifts and callings.

Expectations when the things of God are neglected

See Hag 1:5-6, 9, 16

These folks lived their lives in neglect of the things of God and their expectations were never met. When you neglect the things of God, things which will otherwise be right and concrete expectations become wrong expectations. There are many people whose expectations are not being fulfilled because of their neglect of the things of God. They work hard and make the necessary investments but they can't reap what they normally should. You operate far below your capacities and abilities when you live in neglect for the things of God. Make God's business your priority and things will change for the better.

You must ensure that you are living to please the Lord in order that your expectations be met. He said you should delight yourself in Him and He will grant to you the desires of your heart. The Word says, *"Delight yourself in the Lord and he will give you the desires of your heart"* (Ps 37:4). When you delight yourself in the Lord your expectations will be founded and grounded in Him and as such they will be met.

www.ingramcontent.com/pod-product-compliance
Lightning Source LLC
Chambersburg PA
CBHW020657300426
44112CB00007B/422